THE VICTORIA HISTORY OF HEREFORDSHIRE

EASTNOR

Janet Cooper with contributions from David Whitehead and Sylvia Pinches

VICTORIA
COUNTY
HISTORY

First published 2013
Reprinted 2014

A Victoria County History publication

© The University of London, 2013

ISBN 978 1 905165 96 4

Cover image: *Eastnor Castle, 1840, from a survey by Richard Galliers at Eastnor Castle, reproduced by permission of Mr James Hervey-Bathurst.*

Back cover image: *View from Midsummer Hill towards the obelisk, 2011. Photograph by Janet Cooper.*

Typeset in Minion pro by Emma Bohan

Published with the generous support of a grant
from the Geoffrey Walter Smith Fund of
the Woolhope Naturalists' Field Club.

CONTENTS

LIST OF ILLUSTRATIONS

LIST OF MAPS

FOREWORD

FOR VERY MANY YEARS, our muniments room at Eastnor has held bundles of papers, neatly stacked in wooden cupboards, where they have attracted dust rather than attention. All that suddenly changed when Janet Cooper and her team, Sylvia Pinches and David Whitehead, arrived to write this history of the village as part of the Victoria History of the Counties of England (VCH), which originated from the time of Queen Victoria's Diamond Jubilee in 1897. We were delighted that our documents were finally given the chance of proving their worth for this excellent project, now rededicated to our present Queen, and our own archivist, Hazel Lein, was only too pleased to be involved.

The VCH had started its local work in Ledbury after obtaining Heritage Lottery funding in 2005 and by 2010 had produced two scholarly but approachable volumes on the town: *Ledbury: a market town and its Tudor heritage* and *Ledbury: people and parish before the Reformation*. When Janet offered to cover Eastnor next, I had no hesitation in accepting and offering some financial support. The team appeared regularly and worked hard, deciphering mediaeval Latin and early-English deeds with remarkable enthusiasm, comparing old maps with the Ordnance Survey and replacing everything they removed in a tidy and considerably cleaner state. It was a pleasure to be part of the project.

I am sure that this volume will interest people living locally now and in the future. We are lucky to live in a well-recorded place and to have this insight into how Eastnor became the village it is today. I congratulate Janet Cooper and the VCH on their commitment and dedication to their work, to which the Eastnor book is a worthy testament. I am very grateful to them for undertaking this project.

James Hervey-Bathurst

ACKNOWLEDGEMENTS

THE HISTORY OF Eastnor is the first parish history to be produced for the Victoria County History of Herefordshire, which until now has had only one general volume published in 1908. This revival of the Herefordshire VCH has been made possible by the Trust for the Victoria County History of Herefordshire, founded in 1998. Eastnor was chosen as the first parish to be tackled as it adjoins the borough of Ledbury, the subject of the two paperbacks by Sylvia Pinches written as part of the VCH-sponsored and Heritage Lottery-funded England's Past for Everyone project.

The history, apart from the chapter on Eastnor Castle by David Whitehead, has been written by Janet Cooper, with assistance from Sylvia Pinches on the 19th and 20th centuries. Many others have assisted with the research. In particular, the Herefordshire VCH volunteers have photographed and transcribed the Eastnor wills made between 1500 and 1700, and transcribed the parish registers and the 19th-century census records. Sue Hubbard helped to take notes on deeds at Eastnor Castle, and David Lovelace photographed documents at Eastnor and at the National Archives. C.R.J. Currie generously visited and wrote notes on the architecture of some of the domestic buildings, and J.E.C. Peters, assisted by some of the VCH volunteers, made a study of the farm buildings. John Freeman not only provided information on individual place-names, but also made available some of the English Place-Name Society notes on Eastnor. Brian Smith read and commented on an early draft of the text. They are all sincerely thanked.

The history could not have been written without access to the muniments at Eastnor Castle, and the Trust is most grateful to Mr James Hervey-Bathurst for allowing access to them, and to his archivist Hazel Lein for producing them. The archivists and staff at the Herefordshire Record Office and at Hereford Cathedral Library, and the librarians at Hereford City Library have also been unfailingly helpful and are sincerely thanked.

The Trust is grateful to the Executive Editor of the VCH, Elizabeth Williamson, and her colleagues who have been responsible for the final editing of this book and seeing it through the press.

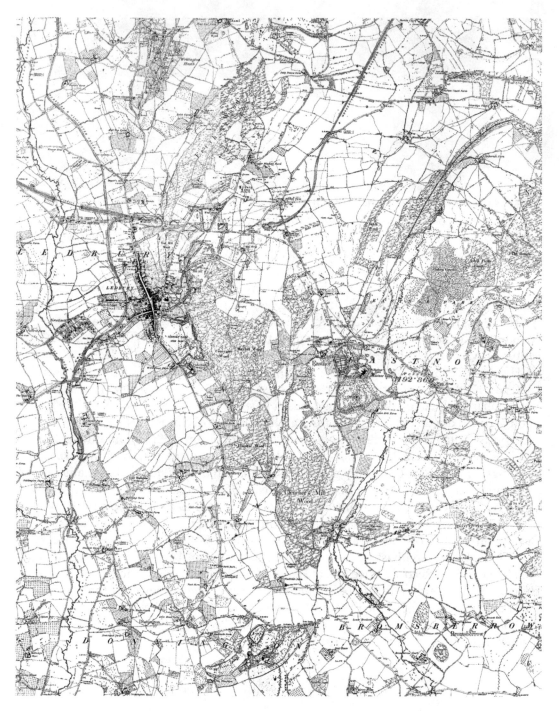

Map 1   *Eastnor and surrounding area in 1892, showing its relationship to Ledbury to the west, to the Malvern Hills marking the boundary with Worcestershire to the north and east, and to Gloucestershire to the south.*

INTRODUCTION

THE SMALL PARISH of Eastnor lies at the southern end of the Malvern Hills, about a mile east of the market town of Ledbury. It is known today for its remarkable Picturesque castle, built in medieval style between 1812 and 1820 by Sir Robert Smirke for John Somers Cocks, third Baron and later first Earl Somers, to replace the earlier manor house called Castleditch. The castle stands near the centre of the parish on a small hill overlooking an ornamental lake and a large deer park beyond. On a hill above the park is an obelisk, erected by Lord Somers in 1811, and bearing on its base memorial inscriptions to the first Lord Somers, lord chancellor to William III (d. 1716), and to Ensign James Cocks, killed in 1758, with an additional inscription to Lord Somers's eldest son, Edward Charles Cocks, killed in action at Burgos (Spain) in 1812.[1]

Parish Boundaries

The roughly square parish covers 1292 ha. (3193 a.). Its position, bounded by Ledbury parish on the west and north and the county boundary on the east and south, suggests that at some time before 1066, when it was first recorded, Eastnor was formed out of the south-east corner of an early, larger Ledbury parish. The name Eastnor, which means the place east of the ridge,[2] was clearly given to the parish by people viewing it from Ledbury. The eastern and southern parish boundaries, the county boundaries with Worcestershire and Gloucestershire, run along the ridge of the Malvern Hills and along the tops of the line of lower hills westwards as far as the Glynch brook at Clencher's Mill.[3] A short section of the eastern boundary follows the earthwork known as the Shire Ditch which may be of prehistoric origin. Part of the southern boundary, between Eastnor and Bromsberrow parish in Gloucestershire, was disputed in 1221.[4] The western and northern boundaries, with Ledbury parish, follow some tracks and field boundaries, but for much of their length run across fields and through woods.[5] The exact course of the northern boundary, which runs almost straight from Lower Mitchell to the Glynch, often seems to have been uncertain. In 1313 land in Little Withycroft field, usually part of Eastnor, was in Ledbury.[6] In 1613 land in Mitchell field, presumably belonging to the

1   National Heritage List 1266786; Eastnor Castle Mun., Smirke plans.
2   B. Coplestone-Crow, *Herefordshire Place-names* (2nd edn, Logaston Press, 2009), 90.
3   OS Maps, 1:10,000 (digitally derived); ibid., Explorer 190; HRO, Q/R1/17 (Eastnor inclosure award).
4   *Rolls of the Justices in Eyre for Gloucestershire, Warwickshire and Staffordshire* (Selden Soc. lix, 1940), p. 101, no. 241.
5   OS Maps, 1:2500, Herefordshire XXXVI, XLII (1930 edn.); HRO, Q/R1/17.
6   DCA 7018/3, p. 16.

hamlet of Mitchell in Ledbury, was in Eastnor parish.[7] In 1649 land in Westbrook field was in Ledbury, but in 1716 other land in that field was in Eastnor.[8] In 1690 and 1779 land in the same area was said to be in the parishes of Eastnor and Ledbury, or one of them.[9] The tenurial and agricultural connections between Eastnor and the small area of Ledbury to its north were close from the early Middle Ages onwards, and the following account covers part of the area known as Mitchell and Massington in Ledbury parish.

Landscape

The Malverns, the dramatic range of hills which mark the county boundary with Worcestershire, dominate the landscape. They were probably an important boundary as early as the Neolithic period. In the Bronze and Iron Ages enclosures, including the fort at Midsummer Hill in Eastnor, were built on them.[10] In the Middle Ages they provided rough grazing and hunting. Under the Malvern Hills Act of 1884, the hills, including 'the attractive hilly parkland of Eastnor' were managed by the Malvern Hills Conservators. The Malverns, including the whole of Eastnor parish, were declared an Area of Outstanding Natural Beauty in 1959.[11] An area of 30 a. on the summit of Midsummer Hill, covering the hillfort there, was given to the National Trust in 1923 by the rector, Revd H.L. Somers-Cocks, in memory of his son Capt. Reginald Somers-Cocks.[12]

The landscape of Eastnor is hilly, cut by the valleys of the Glynch and its tributary streams. The highest ground is on the eastern boundary, along the end of the Malvern Hills, where the land rises steeply to a high point of 284 m. at Midsummer Hill, to 265 m. north of Gullet quarry, and to 254 m. at Ragged Stone Hill to the south. The lower hills along the western boundary rise to 194 m. In the north, Eastnor Hill, the north – south ridge beside the road to Ledbury, rises to 176 m., and the long spur of the ridgeway to its north-east to 143 m. Some of the valleys between the hills fall to c. 100 m., and at Clencher's Mill, on the southern boundary, the land falls to 69 m., the lowest point in the parish.[13] The extensive Castle grounds, with the area around the church, the home farm and the village green became a conservation area in 1992.[14]

The geology is complicated,[15] and the parish is crossed by several fault lines. At its eastern edge, Midsummer, Ragged Stone and Chase End Hills are composed of the hard Pre-Cambrian Malverns Complex rocks which form the high ground of the Malverns and whose soils produce rough grazing. South-west of the hills are outcrops of

7   Eastnor Castle Mun., case 3, unnumbered box, bundle 51 (Whitehouse), no. 1.
8   ibid., case 1, bundle 2, no. 3; case 3, box 1, bundle 60.
9   ibid., case 1, bundle 2, nos. 16, 17; case 3, box 1, bundle 60.
10   M. Bowden, *The Malvern Hills: An ancient landscape* (English Heritage, 2005), 13–15.
11   www.malvernhillsaonb.org.uk/about_the_aonb.html, accessed 9 August 2011.
12   *The Times* 24 April 1923, from digital archive infotrac.galegroup.com, accessed 22 July 2011; plaque at summit.
13   OS Maps 1:10,000 SO 73 NE, SO 73 NW (1973 edn).
14   *Hereford Times*, 10, 17 October 1991; www.herefordshire.gov.uk/housing/planning/29825.asp, accessed 3 February 2012.
15   The following paragraph has been revised by Dr Peter Oliver, Herefordshire & Worcestershire Earth Heritage Trust.

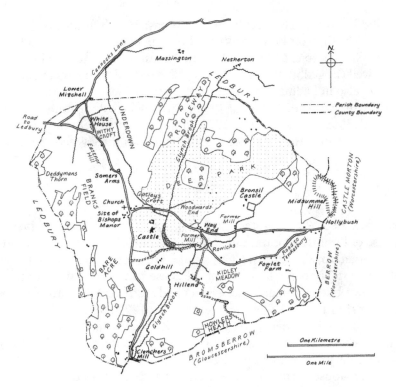

Map 2   *Eastnor parish in 1813, just after the foundation stone of the new castle had been laid. A large area of the parish was already covered by an 18th-century deer park.*

Cambrian sandstones and shales with numerous igneous intrusions of Ordovician age, particularly in the area around Fowlet Farm. Silurian rocks also occur: the high ground in the centre of the parish is composed of May Hill sandstone with a narrow band of Woolhope limestone at its western edge. The hills and ridges near the northern and western boundaries are of Wenlock limestone, the lower ground between them being of poorly draining Wenlock shale. Along all the streams are deposits of head (clay, sand, and gravel); only along the Glynch brook are there also bands of alluvium.[16] The Pre-Cambrian granites and diorites and Cambrian sandstone are good building material, which has been used since some of the sandstone was quarried for Midsummer Hill fort in the 5th century BC.[17]

Several streams rise in the high ground in the north and east of the parish, uniting as the Glynch brook whose valley bisects the southern half of the parish. The brook was dammed just north of the present Eastnor Castle to form a triangular fishpond, recorded on an estate map of 1726.[18] When Eastnor Castle was built between 1812 and 1820 the pond was altered to create the artificial lake which is a feature of the castle grounds. The westernmost stream, seasonal and partly culverted by 1934, rises near Deadwoman's Thorn and flows north to join another brook near Mitchell; it was called Brankswell

16   Geological Survey Map (solid and drift), sheet 216 Tewkesbury (1988 edn).
17   S.C. Stanford, *Midsummer Hill, an Iron-Age hill fort on the Malverns* (1981), 20.
18   Eastnor Castle Mun., Castleditch map 1726.

brook in the Middle Ages.[19] The next brook to the east, which flows past Mitchell, was usually called Withycroft brook or Withy brook between the 14th and the 17th centuries.[20] The Glynch, so called in 1821, is the largest brook;[21] it rises in the Malvern Hills, at Walmswell (in Ledbury parish) below the Herefordshire Beacon, and flows past Netherton Farm, also in Ledbury, before turning south towards Eastnor Castle. It was probably this stream whose diversion in 1591 damaged a road.[22] Another brook, called Kydeles brook in 1356 and Padbrook in 1578 and 1713,[23] rises near the eastern parish boundary and flows south-west past Bronsil Castle to join the Glynch just below the lake at Eastnor Castle.

The Chase and Parks

From the early Middle Ages the eastern part of the parish was within the bishop of Hereford's chase or hunting ground, called the chase of Colwall and Eastnor in 1278. It adjoined the larger, royal, Malvern Chase on the Worcestershire side of the Malvern hills.[24] In 1389 Bishop Trefnant claimed that the chase had been granted to the see by an otherwise unknown but presumably early 'King Meldruth' or Meredith, and confirmed by Pope Innocent II in 1130.[25] Its bounds, recorded in 1277 and 1650, cannot be firmly identified, but the southernmost point in 1650 was 'Chomsford' (Clenchford or Clencher's) Mill, whence the boundary ran to Eastnor church, then to the Ridgeway near the northern boundary of Eastnor, and then to Froglane, which seems to have been near the modern White House Farm. The survey also included within the chase three areas of land in Eastnor: the Gullet between the county boundary and News wood (73 a.), Broad Downs between the Gullett and Colwall parish (*c.* 33 a.), and Shotters Hill (*c.* 51 a.).[26] Both Malvern Chase and the bishop's chase were disafforested under Charles I, and much of the area became common land for the parishes of Eastnor, Colwall and Ledbury, but *c.* 52 a. on or near Midsummer Hill was allotted to the bishop for his see.[27] Entrances to the chase from Eastnor were marked by two 'gates', each the site of a farmstead or hamlet: wood gate at the later Woodwards End, recorded as Woodyate *c.* 1288, and fowl gate, modern Fowlet, first recorded as a surname in the mid 13th century.[28]

19   L. Richardson, *Wells and Springs of Herefordshire* (Memoirs of the Geological Survey, HMSO, 1935), 75; DCA 1726.
20   *TWNFC* (1923), 235, from DCA 3277; Eastnor Castle Mun., Castleditch box.
21   Eastnor Castle Mun., Eastnor Parish box 1, personal survey booklet, p. 7.
22   HRO, AM33/7.
23   ibid., CF50/178, Heref DD 28 (Cal of BL Add Ch 72752); ibid. AA59 A2, f. 102v.; Eastnor Castle Mun., case 2, bundle 2.
24   *Cal. Pat.* 1272–81, 284, 490; *Reg. Trefnant*, 166; B.S. Smith, *Hist. Malvern* (2nd edn, 1978), 27–31.
25   *Reg. Trefnant*, 166; M.G. Watkins, *Collections for the History and Antiquities of Herefordshire, Radlow Hundred* (1902) bound as Duncomb's *Herefordshire* vol. 5, p. 53.
26   *Reg. Trefnant*, 169; TNA, E 320/F24, printed in Watkins, *Collections for the History of Herefordshire, Radlow Hundred*, pp. 84–6.
27   Watkins, *Collections for the History of Herefordshire, Radlow Hundred*, pp. 85–6; HRO, K13/20.
28   HRO, AA59 A1, p. 145; ibid., AH82/5; ibid., CF50/178, Heref DD 15 (Cal of BL Add Ch 72707); BL Add MS 46458, ff. 15, 19.

In 1460 Richard Beauchamp, son of John Beauchamp first baron Beauchamp of Powick, obtained the king's licence to create a 1300-acre deer park on land he had bought in the eastern half of the parish;[29] it centred on a Brome or Bromey hill, a name which became Bronsil. As a settlement of the Bronsil estate in 1469 described only 521 a.,[30] the park presumably extended into the bishop's chase on the Malverns, and indeed the bishop later disputed Beauchamp's right to the park.[31] Bronsil park was recorded in 1544 and 1578,[32] and may still have been in existence in the 1630s,[33] but by 1726 the Bronsil estate comprised only a number of inclosures, one of which was called High Park and contained 20 a. of coarse pasture.[34]

In 1726 a 6-acre pasture close called the Park extended southwards from Castleditch house along the Glynch, but across the river was the 32-acre Great Home meadow or 'Old Park'.[35] The two together may have made up the 50-acre park recorded in 1759, or that park may have been the modern deer park, 90 a. in 1770, which in 1805 contained some very large oaks.[36]

Communications

Two main roads run through Eastnor. The road from Hereford through Ledbury to Malvern and Worcester cuts across the north-west corner of the parish. In the 20th century it was a major road, but earlier it was apparently less important, being called Cannocks Lane in 1726, perhaps from Richard Cannock who had held land near the road in the mid 17th century.[37] It was turnpiked under the Ledbury Roads Act of 1721, and disturnpiked in 1871.[38]

The road from Hereford through Ledbury and Tewkesbury to Cheltenham, the major road in 1726, runs from the Hereford–Worcester road through Eastnor parish from north-west to south-east. It was called the king's road in the 14th century, and the road to Tewkesbury in the 15th.[39] In the 17th century, and presumably earlier, it probably carried goods shipped up the Severn, for in 1696 the inhabitants of Eastnor petitioned parliament against the bill for the Wye and Lugg navigation, claiming that an Act would

29   Below, Settlement, Landownership, Bronsil, for an account of this estate and of Richard Beauchamp, a distant cousin of Richard Beauchamp, earl of Warwick (d. 1439).
30   *Cal. Close. 1468–76*, 459.
31   *Cal. Chart R. 1427–1516*, 137; BL Add MS 72856, f. 7.
32   Eastnor Castle Mun., Bronsil box; HRO, AA59 A2, ff. 95v., 97, 101.
33   Eastnor Castle Mun., Castleditch box: courts of 15 March 1630, 24 July 1638.
34   ibid., Bronsil map 1726; ibid., Bronsil box, undated 18th-century valuation.
35   ibid., Castleditch map 1726, with pencilled annotations.
36   ibid., case 1, bundle 5; ibid., Eastnor Estates box 11, survey by Nathaniel Kent; E. W. Brayley and John Britton, *The Beauties of England and Wales* (1805), vi. 597.
37   Eastnor Castle Mun., 1726 map; ibid., case 1, bundle 2, no. 4; Isaac Taylor, *Map of Herefs.* 1754.
38   *Act for repairing the several roads leading to the town of Ledbury in the county of Hereford*, 7 Geo. I c 3; *Annual Turnpike Acts Continuance Acts*, 33 & 34 Vic c 73, 34 & 35 Vic c 115; HRO, BS96/46.
39   HRO CF50/178, Heref DD 15 (Cal of BL Add Ch 72752), Heref DD 28 (BL Add Ch 72752), Heref H 41 (BL Add Ch 72719), Heref A 11 (BL Add Ch 72848).

do great damage to their parish.[40] Like the Worcester road, the Tewkesbury road was turnpiked in 1721 and disturnpiked in 1871.[41] The road was rebuilt and realigned in 1828, diverting it eastwards and northwards away from the church and the castle and straightening the eastern stretch of the road.[42] The opening of the M50 motorway, from Ross-on-Wye to Tewkesbury in 1960 and to Strensham in 1962,[43] reduced the importance of this road.

Clencher's Mill Lane, now a narrow lane leading south from Eastnor Castle to Bromsberrow, was another king's road in 1380.[44] Other lanes, tracks and footpaths connect Eastnor with Ledbury and the scattered farmsteads of the parish with each other. In 1467 four men paid rent to the bishop's manor for land to improve their 'way', presumably a private access route.[45]

In the 19th century Eastnor was served by carriers travelling from Ledbury to Tewkesbury, men like Levi Clifton of Ledbury whose wagon travelled to Tewkesbury on Wednesdays. Most carriers to Ledbury went on Tuesdays, the town's market day.[46]

By 1927 Midland Red Motors were running a bus service from Hollybush on the eastern parish boundary, through Eastnor to Ledbury on Tuesdays. A similar service was still running in 2012.[47] Another service, run by BC and RJF Pedlingham of Colwall, was taken over by Bristol Tramways in 1932. Buses along the main road from Ledbury to Great Malvern, through the northern edge of Eastnor, were also running by the 1920s and continued in the 1970s.[48] A Saturday service from Ledbury to Tewkesbury through Eastnor ran in 2012.[49]

The Hereford – London railway line cuts through the north-western corner of the parish, but the nearest railway station is at Ledbury, where the line to Hereford and Worcester opened in 1861 and that to Gloucester in 1885.[50]

There was a postal service in 1867 when the parish clerk was sub-postmaster; the main post office being in Ledbury.[51] In 1879 a postman was found guilty of destroying

40   *Journal of House of Commons*, vol. 11 (published 1803), www. british-history.ac.uk, accessed 1 February 2011.
41   *Act for repairing the several roads leading to the town of Ledbury in the county of Hereford*, 7 Geo. I c 3; *Annual Turnpike Acts Continuance Acts*, 33 & 34 Vic c 73, 34 & 35 Vic c 115.
42   Eastnor Castle Mun., Eastnor Parish box 1, 'Personal Survey of Eastnor', p. 10; box 2, unnumbered bundle of papers.
43   www.ciht.org.uk/motorway/m50rossspur.htm, accessed 23 February 2012.
44   HRO, CF50/178, Heref HH 32 (TS Cal of BL Add Ch 72787).
45   BL Add MS 46458, f. 6.
46   S. Pinches, *Ledbury, A Market Town and its Tudor Heritage* (Phillimore, 2009), 112; unpublished article on Ledbury Carriers by John Harrison.
47   J. Harrison, unpublished article on Ledbury Carriers, citing Tilley's *Ledbury Almanac*; J.E. Dunabin, *The Hereford Bus* (H I Publications, 1985), 36; www.herefordshirecouncil.gov.uk/docs/publictransport, accessed 3 February 2012.
48   C.J. Davis, *Round the Hills: an account of 70 years of Bus Services in the Malverns* (Omnibus Soc., 1979), 17–18, 20, 37.
49   www.herefordshire.gov.uk/transport-and-highways/public-transport/travelling-by-bus, accessed 3 February 2012.
50   J. Hillaby, *Ledbury: a medieval borough* (2nd edn, Logaston Press, 2005), 110.
51   Littlebury's *Dir. Herefs.* (1867); Slater's *Dir. Herefs.* (1868); inf. from Mr Alan Starkey who gave assistance with the postal history.

letters at the office.[52] By 1871 the post office was next to the school house, in the 17th-century cottage the postmistress occupied at the time of the office's closure in 2001.[53] Early in the 20th century a small office, incorporating a letter box of the reign of Edward VII (1901–10) was added on the western end of the cottage. In 1963 the 85 year-old postmistress celebrated 60 years of running the office, and the postmistress in 2001 had been there 21 years.[54]

Public Services

Springs, streams and private wells supplied water to Eastnor until the later 20th century.[55] In 1898 the Eastnor estate provided a new water supply to the village, and Lady Henry Somerset of Eastnor Castle built a well or fountain, covered with a pyramidal tiled roof, on the small triangular green near the Castle gates. The brick wall behind the modern tap is decorated with terracotta reliefs depicting Christ and the Samaritan woman at the well and two angels.[56] The water was piped, presumably from Walmswell below the Herefordshire Beacon, which provided much of the parish's water in 1923. In 1930 and 1931 a new reservoir was built there to augment the supply.[57] The Herefordshire Water Board's mains were extended into the village in 1963, and along the lane past the castle as far as St Mary's Home, later Birchams Grange, in 1965.[58]

Drainage is supplied to the village by the Eastnor Estate.[59] Mains electricity reached the parish in the early 1930s. There is no gas supply.[60]

The Impact of National Events

Although the modern Eastnor Castle was not built until 1812, its predecessor, Castleditch, first recorded as an unfree tenement *c.* 1288, took its name from a castle ditch.[61] The site is too far from Midsummer Hill for the name to derive from the defences there. Perhaps, as happened at nearby Castlemorton (Worcs.),[62] a castle was built in the 12th century. Such a castle, presumably built for the bishop of Hereford, would have commanded the Tewkesbury road where it crossed the Glynch and thus have protected

52 *Ledbury Free Press*, 4 Nov. 1879.
53 TNA, RG 10/2682; *Ledbury Reporter*, 29 June 2001.
54 Eastnor Castle Mun., box on local life; *Hereford Times*, 5 April 1963; inf. from Mr. Alan Starkey.
55 TNA, MAF 37/8/153.
56 HRO, M5B/15/3; Eastnor Castle Mun., box on local life; www.imagesofengland.org.uk, accessed 20 January 2012.
57 H. L Somers-Cocks, *Eastnor and Its Malvern Hills* (Hereford 1923), 167; Eastnor Castle Mun., Eastnor Estates box 15; Richardson, *Wells and Springs of Herefordshire*, 75.
58 HRO, BB32/23/2, 5.
59 Inf. from Mr James Hervey-Bathurst.
60 HRO, HD10, 1932 box: faculty to install electric light in the church; Kelly's *Dir. Herefs.* (1937–41).
61 David N. Parsons and Tania Styles, *The Vocabulary of English Place-Names: Brace – Cæster*, 145–7.
62 *VCH Worcs.* iv: http://www.british-history.ac.uk/report.aspx?compid=42854, accessed 14 November 2011.

Ledbury against attack from the east during the civil war of the 1140s. Presumably the castle did not long survive.

In the Middle Ages the chase and its game were a temptation to some local men. John the parker of Eastnor was among those whom Hugh le Despenser, lord of Hanley Castle (Worcs.) and its chase, accused in 1338 and 1340 of hunting in Malvern Chase and carrying off his deer.[63] In 1524 another man was fined for killing a buck in the bishop's chase.[64] The motive for other disturbances is less clear. In 1417 an Eastnor ploughman and a Bosbury man were pardoned for the murder of John Milward, possibly committed during a more general outbreak of violence. Two labourers and a husbandman from Eastnor were to be arrested in 1448.[65]

Eastnor was briefly involved in the Civil War. Early in 1644 Castleditch was taken by a small Parliamentarian force, but was quickly retaken by Royalists from Hereford. Lead bullets, said to be from these engagements, remained embedded in the door of Castleditch house until its demolition in the early 19th century.[66] The action probably extended to Bronsil Castle which was said in the later 17th century to have been burnt during the war.[67]

63   *Cal. Pat.* 1338–40, 183.
64   HRO, AM33/15.
65   *Cal. Pat.* 1416–22, 103–4; ibid. 1467–77, 102.
66   John Webb, *Memoirs of the Civil War in Herefordshire*, ii. 123; D. Ross, *Royalist, But* (Logaston Press, 2012), 86–7; G.H. Piper, 'Bronsil Castle, Eastnor', *TWNFC* (1880), 231.
67   HRO, CF10/96, p. 308.

SETTLEMENT AND POPULATION

Prehistoric Settlement

THERE WAS SOME NEOLITHIC activity in the extreme south of the parish, around Clencher's Mill and Howler's Heath, where field walking has found scattered flints.[1] The main focus of later prehistoric settlement was at Midsummer and Hollybush Hills, on the eastern boundary of the parish, where a few possibly Neolithic flint implements and a number of Beaker sherds have been found. Traces survive of what may have been a late Bronze-Age hill-top enclosure and, to the north, a Bronze-Age barrow.[2]

In the Iron Age the two hills were surrounded by a double rampart to create a hill fort, extensively excavated between 1965 and 1970. Unusually, the fort had a water supply from a spring in the gully between the two hills. Inside the rampart evidence has been found for between 442 and 526 hut platforms, some of them on steeply sloping ground. Pottery finds included salt containers from Droitwich, and at least some of the iron ore worked on the site came from the Forest of Dean. The excavator's suggested population of *c.* 2,000 for the hill fort seems excessive, particularly in view of the proximity of the contemporary fort on the Herefordshire Beacon; presumably a high proportion of the huts were used for storage. The huts were burnt down in the early to mid 1st century AD, possibly during the Roman invasion, and settlement seems to have shifted to lower ground, near the modern Martins Farm where field walking has revealed a concentration of Roman pottery sherds.[3]

Population from 1086

From the Middle Ages onwards settlement in the parish has been scattered, mainly on the lower ground near the streams, and comparatively sparse. The place-name Brankswell, which is derived from the Old Welsh personal name Branog,[4] suggests the presence of a Welshman in the parish in the early Middle Ages, perhaps as late as the 11th or 12th century. In 1086 there were at least 21 tenants, who would have been heads of household, on Eastnor manor; assuming an average household size of 4.5, the total population would have been 90–100.[5] About 1288 there were 49 tenants and

1   HER 5350, 5354.
2   S.C. Stanford, *Midsummer Hill*, 118–20, 137–8, 163; HER 7150, 7357; M. Bowden, *The Malvern Hills*, 15.
3   Stanford, *Midsummer Hill*, 116–17, 132, 149, 153, 168; HER 931, 7355.
4   DCA 584; inf. from John Freeman.
5   *Domesday Book, Herefordshire* (Phillimore) 2, 27 (f. 182).

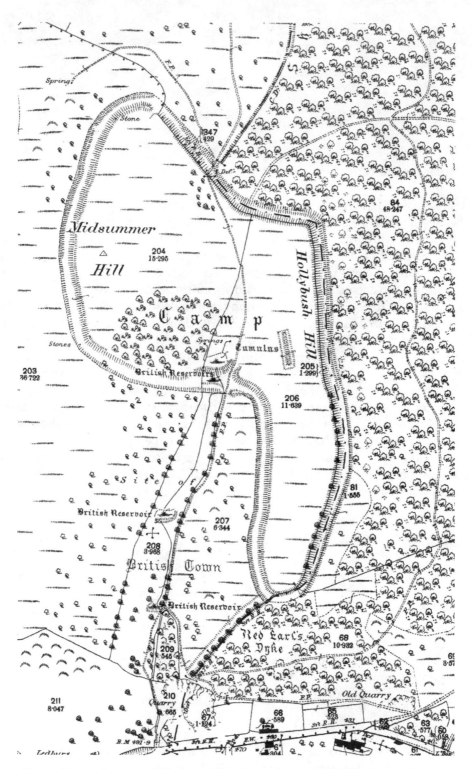

Map 3   *The prehistoric fort on Midsummer Hill, at the southern end of the Malvern Hills.*

their families on the bishop's manor,[6] which still covered most of the parish; this figure suggests that, allowing for a few tenants on other estates, the total population of the parish may have been *c*. 250. The grant in 1379 of an 'unbuilt messuage', presumably the site of a former house, beside a road in Eastnor, may indicate the usual declining population after the famines and plagues of the 14th century; in 1497 several tenements were in the lord's hands and the bailiff could not find out who should pay rent for them.[7] Recovery was not complete in 1577, and in 1578 a total of 25 named tenants held 27 'built messuages', 13 messuages, and 3 cottages as well as 6 'unbuilt messuages'.[8] Forty-one people were assessed for hearth tax in 1665;[9] if, as is likely, they were all heads of households, that would suggest a total population in excess of 200, as the list excludes those exempt by poverty. However, the Compton census of 1676 recorded 107 adults in the parish,[10] which, allowing for children, would imply a population of 150–160. Baptismal numbers suggest a slight increase in the late 17th and the early 18th century. The population presumably grew quickly in the mid and late 18th century, for in 1801 it was 384. It continued to rise, to a peak of 500 in 1851. For much of the period 1871–1951 it hovered around 400, although in 1901 it reached 491 (including a household of 18 at the castle and 27 people at St Mary's Home for girls). Thereafter it fell steadily, to 457 in 1921, to 333 in 1961, and to 289 in 2001. In 2011 the combined population of Eastnor and the adjoining parish of Donnington was 339.[11]

Medieval and Later Settlement

Like much of Herefordshire, Eastnor, although it had an open-field system, was a parish of hamlets and scattered farmsteads.[12] The small modern village between the church and the castle, earlier called Church End, was not recorded until 1578 when William Weobley held a 'built messuage' there. In 1726 the rectory house and three small houses stood near the church.[13] There were six houses or cottages there in 1841 and 1851. Only in 1861, when there were 11 households there, was the area called the village.[14] The former post office, originally built in the late 17th century but extended since, survives on the corner of the main road opposite the main gates to the castle.

Way End on the Tewkesbury road was probably the largest settlement in the parish until the mid 19th century. The name first occurs as the surname borne by three people

6   HRO, AA59 A1, pp. 143–7.
7   ibid., CF50/178, Heref HH 33 (Cal of BL Add Ch 72785); ibid., AM33/12. There are no figures for the poll tax.
8   HRO, AA59 A2, ff. 92–103.
9   HRO Libr., TS transcript of 1665 Hearth Tax by J. Harnden, pp. 73–4.
10   *Compton Census*, ed. A. Whiteman (British Academy, 1986), 260.
11   *Census*, 1801–1991 www.herefordshire.gov.uk/factsandfigures/subcounty.aspx, accessed 1 February 2012, 9 March 2013.
12   For fields, below, Economic History, Agriculture; on dispersed and nucleated settlement in Herefordshire, R.E. Skelton, 'Herefordshire: the evidence for and against medieval dispersed settlement', *TWNFC* (2011), 27–55.
13   HRO, AA59 A2, f. 96.; Eastnor Castle Mun., Castleditch map 1726.
14   TNA, HO 107/424/13; HO 107/1975, f. 82v.; ibid., RG 9/1808, f. 84 and v.

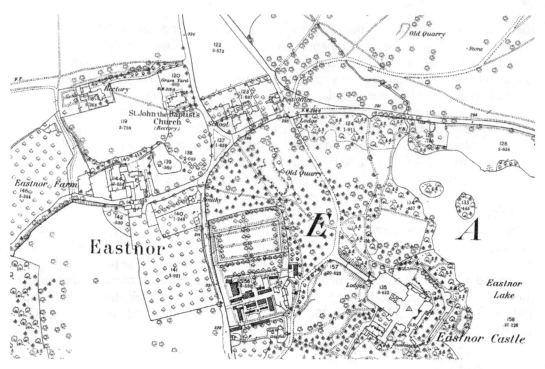

Map 4   *Map showing Eastnor village in 1892, with church, rectory house, and school close to the Castle grounds, and to the home farm of the estate.*

listed in the rental of the bishop's manor *c.* 1288.[15] Two adjoining messuages there were sold in 1610.[16] Three houses were shown there on the Castleditch estate map of 1726, with a further two at the nearby Rowick;[17] at least one other surviving 17th-or early 18th-century house was not shown on the estate map. There were 11 houses or cottages there in 1841, making it the biggest settlement in the parish, but by 1851 there were only six occupied houses.[18] Almost adjoining Way End on the south-east was another small settlement. Two men surnamed Rowyke, probably meaning 'rough farm', held of the bishop *c.* 1288.[19] In 1713 a house adjoined Rowick Green,[20] as did the Rowicks Farm shown on the 1726 map. A small group of timber-framed houses, of 17th-century origin, survives at Wayend Street and along the lane leading to the former Rowicks Farm; below them are two 20th-century semi-detached estate cottages.

The second element of the name Bokbury or Bukbury, recorded occasionally between the 13th and the 15th centuries, (*burh* meaning an enclosure, almost always for a house or houses) suggests that it was the site of an important early house.[21] However, there is

15   HRO, AA59 A1, pp. 143–4, 146–7.
16   Eastnor Castle Mun., case 2, bundle 2.
17   ibid., Castleditch map 1726.
18   TNA, HO 107/424/13; HO 107/1975, f. 81v.
19   HRO, AA59 A1, p. 146; *Place-Name Elements* ii. (EPNS xxvi, 1956), 88.
20   Eastnor Castle Mun., case 2, bundle 2.
21   DCA 1741; ibid. 7018/1, p. 3; BL Add Ch 72743 (reference supplied by John Freeman from EPNS notes).

no evidence for any settlement in Branksfield in the north-west quarter of the parish where Bukbury lay. The nearby Gatelithe, later Gateley, recorded as a surname from the mid 12th century, was the centre of a medieval freehold estate. The name, which derives from 'goat' and OE *hlith*, meaning a slope, particularly a concave hillside, suits a site on Eastnor Hill at or close to the later Somers Arms and near the 19th-century Gatleys Croft.[22] The surname is recorded throughout the Middle Ages and the 16th century, and one of the houses was recorded, as Gatlers End, in 1806.[23]

There may have been another small settlement near a meadow called the Homme. The surname de Homme occurs from the early 13th century, and was borne by one of the medieval freeholders *c.* 1288.[24] The descent of the freehold suggests that the Homme was near the present Castle, where there was a Ham meadow in 1606.[25]

Three or four men surnamed de Sothinton (the south farm or settlement) witnessed deeds in the mid 13th century.[26] The surname continued in the 14th century,[27] and land in Sothintone in the manor of Eastnor was sold in 1337.[28] As its name suggests, the settlement was in the south of the parish, probably near Clencher's Mill where there was a small group of cottages in 1816.[29] There were still nine cottages at Clencher's Mill and five in Clencher's Mill Wood in the mid 19th century.[30]

Other small settlements included Woodgate or Wood End where there were two messuages in 1549 and in 1578.[31] One had probably gone by 1715 when one tenement with two gardens there was conveyed to Thomas Cocks of Castleditch, and the site was occupied by a large farmhouse and outbuildings in 1726.[32] Three men surnamed 'Styweye' occur in 1313 and 1314, and another in 1346,[33] but Styweys was among the lands emparked by Richard Beauchamp in 1460, and by the late 15th century only a toft, probably the site of a lost house, remained at Stywayend.[34] Howler's Heath, in its medieval form Oulithe (owl's hill), also gave rise to a medieval surname, first recorded in the mid 13th century; three people surnamed 'of Oulithe' appear in the *c.* 1288 rental.[35] A messuage and a croft at Ouleth were excluded from a conveyance in 1399. There were

22 HRO, AH82/3; ibid., Q/R1/17; Coplestone-Crow, *Herefordshire Place-names*, 91; for the estate see below, Landownership, Goodings.

23 *Hereford Journal*, July 1806: reference supplied by Ms Jean Currie.

24 HRO, AH82/6; ibid., AA59 A1, p. 143. Some of the Eastnor men surnamed Homme may have taken their name from the Homme in Ledbury, see DCA 1748.

25 Eastnor Castle Mun., Castleditch box. There was also an Old Hom at Fowlet in 1578: HRO, AA59 A2, f. 95 and v. For the freehold, later manor, see below, Landownership, Castleditch.

26 HRO, AH82/4, AH82/6, AH82/7, ibid., G37/II/87; DCA 1889,

27 e.g. HRO, CF50/178, Heref DD 9 (TS Cal of BL Add Ch 72720).

28 *Cat Anc.* D. vi. C. 4857.

29 HRO, CF50/178, Heref DD 19 (TS Cal of BL Add Ch 72733); ibid. Q/R1/17; Eastnor Castle Mun., case 2, bundle 1B.

30 TNA, HO 107/424/13; ibid., RG 9/1808, f. 77 and v.

31 HRO, B049 (microfilm of Longleat House MS41); ibid., AA59 A2, ff. 95, 96.

32 Eastnor Castle Mun., case 2, bundle 1A; Castleditch map 1726.

33 HRO, CF50/178, Heref H 44 (Cal of Talbot/Shrewsbury deed), Heref C 32 (Cal of BL Add Ch 7273); BL Add Ch 72704 (reference kindly supplied by John Freeman from EPNS notes).

34 ibid. CF50/178, Heref F 28 (Cal of BL Add Ch 72851); *Cal. Chart R.* vi (1427–1516), 137; BL Add MS 46458, ff.19 v.–20.

35 HRO, AH82/7; ibid., AA59 A1, p. 143.

still at least two houses at Oulithe *c.* 1500, and Owlers tenement was sold to John Cocks in 1757.[36]

The eastern edge of the parish is poorly documented, but three 17th-century cottages survive at Hollybush on the border with Castlemorton (Worcs.). In 1851 there were three cottages at Whiteleaved Oak below Ragged Stone Hill on the boundary with Bromsberrow (Glos.), and seven at Hollybush;[37] both settlements extended into the neighbouring parishes.

Some of the lands attached to settlements on or just over the northern parish boundary in Ledbury parish, lay in Eastnor. The most important, or at least the highest status, settlement was at Massington. The name, which survives as Massington Farm in Ledbury, was recorded as a surname, *c.* 1233, and as a place-name in 1242.[38] The settlement had its own fields by the later 13th century.[39] In the rental of *c.* 1288 it was divided between two estates, both held by knight service,[40] and so presumably with subtenants. In 1393 Massington was called a township.[41] Ten men were assessed for subsidy there in 1524 and 1525, but only eight in 1545 and six in 1547.[42] In 1630 five men paid rent for land in Massington manor.[43] By 1665 Massington was probably part of Mitchell township for administrative purposes.

Northinton was first recorded, as a surname, in 1221; it was a vill separate from Eastnor *c.* 1240.[44] About that date Roger of Northinton dealt with lands above Salter's well, in Withycroft and towards Brankswell 'sitch' or stream,[45] all in the north-west corner of Eastnor parish. A meadow in Northinton and a rent from Northinton hill, also probably in the north-west of the parish, were given to St Katherine's hospital, Ledbury, in the mid 13th century.[46] A charter of *c.* 1270 distinguishes the fee of Roger of Northinton from both Eastnor and Massington, suggesting that the settlement may have been in the area later called Mitchell. Northinton was last recorded in the early 14th century, and its name had been lost by the 15th century. At least part of its area was absorbed into an estate centred on Netherton Farm, further to the east in Ledbury parish.[47]

Netherton itself first occurs in a later medieval copy of a late 13th-century deed conveying a tenement in Eastnor and Netherton, and as a surname in an early 14th-

---

36   BL Add MS 46458, f. 15 and v.; Eastnor Castle Mun., case 2, bundle 2.
37   TNA, HO 107/1975, ff. 76v.–77.
38   DCA 7018/1/1, p. 41 (the witness list is illegible in the original deed, DCA 3696); *Cur. Reg. R.* xvi, no. 2013, p. 411.
39   DCA 7018/3, pp. 10–11.
40   HRO, AA59/A/1, p. 133.
41   TNA, CP 25/1/83/50, number 58, www.medievalgenealogy.org.uk/fines/abstracts/CP_25_1_83_57. shtml#9, accessed 8 January 2010.
42   M.A. Faraday, *Herefordshire taxes in the reign of Henry VIII* (Woolhope Club, Hereford, 2005), pp. 71, 106, 311, 370.
43   Eastnor Castle Mun., Castleditch box.
44   *Rolls of the Justices in Eyre for Gloucestershire, Warwickshire and Staffordshire* (Selden Soc. lix), p. 101, no. 241; DCA 7018/3, p. 21.
45   DCA 3674. For 'sitch', see H.D.G. Foxall, *Shropshire Field-Names* (Shrops. Archaeological Soc. 1980), 6, 19.
46   DCA 1763; ibid. 7018/1, pp. 3–5.
47   ibid., 7018/1, pp. 10–11; 7018/3, pp. 18–20.

century deed.[48] A 1390 rental of St Katherine's hospital land named ten tenants at Netherton, one of whom had to enclose a meadow belonging to Colwall.[49] A terrier (description) of Netherton in 1621 tells of scattered parcels of land in fields and meadows straddling the whole northern boundary between Eastnor and Ledbury; the only dwellings were two cottages, one of them newly built.[50] By 1812 Netherton had probably been reduced to the farmhouse which survived in 2012.[51]

House platforms and ridge and furrow can be seen south-east of Lower Mitchell Farm, just within Eastnor parish.[52] The place called Mitchell, recorded from 1388 and which had its own fields, was in Ledbury parish, but in 1690 a cottage there had lands in Eastnor, Ledbury and Colwall.[53] Seventeen people were assessed for hearth tax in Mitchell in 1665.[54] In 1726 there were nine houses on the Cocks family's estate: four at Upper Mitchell, two near Lower Mitchell, one south-west of Upper Mitchell, and two at and near White House farm in Eastnor. By 1813 only the farmhouses and seven cottages, scattered over the area of Ledbury north of Eastnor, remained.[55]

DOMESTIC BUILDINGS

Buildings before 1800

Drawings on the Castleditch estate map of 1726 suggest that all the houses on the estate, except Castleditch House itself, were then timber-framed.[56] Seventeenth-century inventories regularly record halls, parlours and kitchens with chambers over at least some of them. The smallest such house was that of a labourer, Henry Tomkins, whose probate inventory of 1664 lists only a hall and chamber with a solar above the hall; it was perhaps the house, then occupied by Richard Tomkins, which was assessed on one hearth in 1665. The house of John Weobley, a yeoman and carpenter who died in 1665, was similarly assessed on only one hearth, although it contained an entry or porch with a room over it, and a hall, kitchen and buttery with chambers over them as well as a little buttery. At the other end of the social scale, the gentleman Humphrey Morton at his death in 1671 occupied a house of two storeys with attics containing a hall, parlour and kitchen, with four chambers above them as well as a cellar with a chamber over it; the house was assessed on five hearths, with one stopped up, in 1665.[57]

48 DCA 7018/3, p. 19; HRO, CF50/178, Heref I 35 (Cal of BL Add Ch 72701).
49 DCA 7018/2, p. 87.
50 Eastnor Castle Mun., case 4.
51 DCA 3600; Eastnor Castle Mun., case 1, bundle 12.
52 HER 3773, 5962.
53 BL Add MS 15555, ff. 2v.–3, 5; Eastnor Castle Mun., case 1, bundle 2, nos. 16, 17.
54 HRO Libr., TS transcript of 1665 hearth tax, by J. Harnden.
55 Eastnor Castle Mun., Mitchell map 1726; HRO, Q/R1/25.
56 Eastnor Castle Mun., Castleditch map 1726.
57 HRO, 5/1/37: inventory of Henry Tomkins 1664; ibid., 8/3/14: will of John Webley, 1665; ibid., 29/1/44: will of Humphrey Morton, 1671; ibid., TS transcript of 1665 hearth tax by J. Harnden.

Figure 1 *The Old Post Office, a 17th-century house typical of the older houses surviving in the village.*

Most of the surviving older houses in the parish originally date from the 17th century, although they have been enlarged, and are timber-framed; the infill, presumably originally wattle and daub, is now brick or plaster. Nearly all lie along the line of the former Ledbury to Tewkesbury road or Clencher's Mill Lane.[58] Most of the cottages were two-roomed, of one storey with attics or two storeys, although Tinker's Grove Cottage in Eastnor Park, formerly Woodwards End Farm, is of two storeys with a cellar; all were presumably originally thatched, although many are now tiled. Martins Farm, south of the present Tewkesbury road, seems to have been built in the mid 17th century as an L-plan house, but was enlarged and made square later in the century; it is largely timber-framed but the south front is of stone rubble.

Of the larger, higher status, houses, the earliest are probably Eastnor Farm, the home farm of the Eastnor estate which stands on the site of the bishop's manor, and Goldhill Farm, the farmhouse for a freehold estate.[59]

Eastnor Farm

The earliest part is a timber-framed, east–west cross-wing, probably of the 16th century, which presumably flanked an early hall, perhaps to the south. It includes ceiling beams with very wide chamfers and diagonally-cut stops. In the early 17th century any hall in that position was replaced by a single, two-storeyed, timber-framed bay, and two further such bays were added north of the earlier crosswing. All three bays have dormer gables

---

58   RCHME, *Herefordshire*, ii. 74; English Heritage Archives, RCHME record cards.
59   Except where otherwise stated the following architectural descriptions are by C.R.J. Currie.

on one end, creating a four-gabled west front. The two northern bays were connected to the cross-wing on the ground floor by a door towards the west end of the wall, later moved eastwards, and still later blocked. There are longitudinal ceiling beams with chamfers having scroll stops at their north ends. Between the two bays, rising through both storeys, is a large post with very wide chamfers, which may be reused from an earlier building. In the 19th century the south and east fronts were rebuilt with brick on the lower storey and new brick-nogged timber-framing on the upper storey, with four gables on the east front matching the earlier ones on the west. The west front has single-storeyed, lean-to additions of the 19th century.[60]

To the west, behind the house, is a range of farm buildings, mainly of stone with brick facings, erected by the Eastnor estate in the mid 19th century. The large, covered, cattle-yard is dated 1864; adjoining it on the west is a two-storey range whose lofty, well-lit upper room appears to have been an estate workshop.[61]

Goldhill Farm

The earliest part of Goldhill Farm, originally south-facing, is the centre range, which was timber-framed with a cross passage and at least two bays to the west of it. What may be the head beam of a 16th-century screens passage survives, but otherwise the framing is wholly of the later 17th century, of two storeys and lofts; the house was one-and-a-half rooms deep. One roof truss of this phase may also survive. Before 1726 the house was cased in brick and extended to create an H-plan, with an east wing of four bays with two principal rooms on each floor and a west wing which seems to have been left incomplete at its north end. In the east wing the principal rooms had corner fireplaces, and the south room on the ground floor is fully panelled with raised and fielded panels and bolection-moulded cornices and detail. A cellar under the east wing may date from the same period. The house may have been intended to face north at that time, as the entry to the central block was converted into a hall, from the south side of which rises a framed staircase with turned balusters, close strings and shallow-moulded handrail. The original brickwork includes platbands between the storeys and segmental-headed sash windows. In the 19th century a single-storeyed polygonal bay window of brick, with a dentilled cornice, was added to the south front, blocking the south door to the entrance hall. Probably late in that century the north end of the west wing was extended to match the east wing. The existing roof of the central range was probably reconstructed in the 19th century; it may have been at that time that the gables shown on the wings in a drawing of 1726 were replaced with hips. In the early 21st century bat lofts were created in the lofts over the wings.

60   It has not been possible to examine the roof.
61   Description based on J.E.C. Peters, unpublished report on Eastnor farm buildings; below, Economic History, Agriculture, Farms.

Figure 2 *The earliest part of Hillend Cottages, once a single house, lies at the far end and has larger panels of timber-framing. The smarter north end was built about 30–40 years later.*

Hillend Cottages

Formerly a single house, it was owned and presumably built by the Higgins family, descendants of the Clintons of Castleditch, in the early 17th century.[62] The earliest part of the house is the west cross-wing, perhaps late 16th-century, of two storeys, with an axial chimney stack with triple diagonally-set flues with oversailing courses at the top. There may have been a hall range to the east. In the 17th century, perhaps *c.* 1630, the hall was replaced by the surviving symmetrically-fronted timber-framed main range, facing north, of two storeys and attics, with a central two-storeyed porch between hall and parlour, and an internal stack towards the rear wall. The front has close-studding and had large horizontal windows on both floors, and the first floor and attic each have shallow jetties at the front, that of the attic having a continuous fascia-board with double ovolo mouldings. The door-head of the porch has incised leaf detail, and the jambs and outer head are enriched with double ovolo mouldings. In the late 17th century the windows were replaced by leaded casements with beaded mullions and transoms.

Probably in the 18th century, the entire house was re-roofed with cranked inner principals supporting a classical king-post superstructure. It was perhaps at that time that the wing was heightened and given a projecting fascia to match that of the south range, though without mouldings. In the mid 19th century the house was divided into

62   Eastnor Castle Mun., case 2, bundle B.

three cottages. [63] The staircase in no. 2 has turned balusters, closed strings and an almost flat handrail, but may be a copy of an 18th-century original.

Former Somers Arms

The former inn, now the offices of Roger Oates Design, stands on or near the site of a medieval freehold once held by the Gateley family.[64] In 1792 the house, then the farmhouse of the Lowes Hurst estate, was in a poor state of repair, and it was almost entirely rebuilt soon afterwards, presumably by Lord Somers who acquired the estate in 1793.[65] The main house is of three bays, with two storeys and an attic, built of brick with a plain tiled roof and brick modillion cornice. To the north is a two-bay lower wing, of a single storey and attic, whose brickwork is contemporary with the main block; within it is a timber-framed partition wall, perhaps the rear wall of an earlier house. The front portion of the main house is early 19th-century, with a larger late 19th-century extension to the rear. The eastern range of the outbuildings behind the house is possibly 18th-century, and originally provided stables and carthouse. It was later extended to the west to provide more stables and a coach-house or early garage. A further large stable was added, south of the main house, in the later 19th century.

Nineteenth-Century Buildings

The dominance of the Cocks, later Somers Cocks, family and their Eastnor estate was reflected in 19th- and 20th-century building work.[66] From the early 19th century, the estate craftsmen, directed by the long-lived steward, George Watson, as well as members of the Somers Cocks family, espoused the 'village picturesque' developed by Uvedale Price in his 'Essay on Architecture' (1810).[67] This created a vernacular signature which was apparent in work on all the estate cottages, where patch, mend and enhance was the *leitmotif* rather than demolition and reconstruction. There are some notable examples in the village itself where a copious thatch is allowed to overhang the body of the Old Post Office cottage in a manner that became a fashionable item in the work of the Regency architect, John Nash. Bronsil Cottage, with its veranda and treillage, was in the 1820s the epitome of a cottage fit for a Jane Austen heroine; it was given its romantic appearance by the estate craftsmen in 1818-19. The ruins of Bronsil castle immediately to the east added to its attractions.[68] A pair of Tudor Gothic rubble cottages with freestone dressings was built on the north-east side of the village green in about the 1840s.[69] Towards the end of the century Lady Henry Somerset embarked on a campaign of repairs to the existing

63 TNA, RG 10/2682, f. 7; RG 13/2470, f. 85.
64 Eastnor Castle Mun., Castleditch map 1726; for the freehold, below, Landownership, Goodings.
65 Eastnor Castle Mun., case 1, bundles 4, 7.
66 The following paragraph is by David Whitehead.
67 Price was a regular visitor to Eastnor: 'Letters of Uvedale Price', ed. C. Watkins and B. Cowell, *Walpole Society*, 68 (2006), pp. 53, 59, 92, 258.
68 Eastnor Castle Mun., General Accounts, 3; for the footprint of the house see Map 5 below, Landownership, Bronsil.
69 National Heritage List 1156683.

cottages. In the 1890s she began to add new cottages to the village;[70] some were rather unimaginative but others were reminiscent of the work of fashionable Arts and Crafts architects like Philip Webb and C.F.A. Voysey, who designed a house for Lady Henry at Woodford (Essex) in 1904. Other buildings of the era include St Mary's Home for Girls (1898–9) and a new village well or pump (*c*. 1898–9), both by Edmund Fisher, and a village hall (1912).[71] Hillend, a large, redbrick house, in late 17th- or early 18th-century style, was built in 1910 to the designs of C.H. Biddulph-Pinchard for the agent of the Eastnor estate.[72]

Bronsil House

The former Bronsil Cottage, was the largest of the houses built by the estate; remodelled several times it stands close to Bronsil Castle.[73] Its north-east range probably incorporates

Figure 3 *The Picturesque Bronsil Cottage from the south, c. 1830, showing the polygonal bay window and pretty details obscured later by additions.*

70   e.g. HRO, M5B/15/3.
71   Eastnor Castle Mun., Eastnor Parish box, copy of an undated and unattributed essay of *c*. 1980 on the 'Growth of the Village', pp. 30–4; Brooks and Pevsner, *Herefordshire* (2012), 219; above, Introduction, public services for the well.
72   National Heritage List 1156661; Brooks and Pevsner, *Herefordshire*, 222.
73   The following description is by C.R.J. Currie.

part of the north–south range of the U-plan building shown on a map of 1808. In the early 19th century another building, of stone rubble with brick quoins, probably a stable block, was built to the west. Not long afterwards the house was enlarged and remodelled as a residence for the land agent, George Watson, who was living there by 1820.[74] The stone rubble outbuilding was remodelled to include domestic accommodation, its sash windows with new brick surrounds, and extended towards the earlier building by a south cross-wing of brick with a polygonal south-facing bay window. Apparently in the 1840s a large stuccoed double-depth south block was built, partly obscuring the earlier bay window, itself having a large double-storeyed bay window to the south; at the same time the first smaller house was joined to the main one. In 1891 and 1892 further enlargements were made, to plans by G.H. Godsell, for the new tenant C.W. Bell.[75] A porch was added to the north-east of the 1840s block, creating a continuous east front; inside, on the south wall, is a timber, Jacobean-style fireplace dated 1891. The early, north-east block was remodelled and given a hipped roof, projecting upper storey with tile-hanging that continues on to the porch, two symmetrically placed pairs of windows on the ground floor, and a central doorway, since blocked. Apparently at the same time, a single-storeyed polygonal bay window was added in front of the 1840s bay. In the early 20th century the house was extended at the rear.

LANDOWNERSHIP

Eastnor Manor

Eastnor belonged to the bishop of Hereford in 1066, when it was one of a group of adjoining manors which the bishop held along the western and southern slopes of the Malverns.[76] By the late Middle Ages it had two sub-manors, Goodings and Castleditch, created from earlier estates. The bishops retained Eastnor manor until 1785 when Bishop James Beauclerk exchanged it with Charles Cocks of Castleditch, first Baron Somers of Evesham, for land in Little Marcle.[77] The manor descended with the barony from Charles (d. 1806) to his son John Somers Cocks, first Earl and second Baron Somers (d. 1841) to his son John, second earl and third baron (d. 1852) and to his son Charles, third earl and fourth baron (d. 1883). On Charles's death the Eastnor manor and estate passed to his daughter Isabella Caroline, Lady Henry Somerset (d. 1921).[78] It then reverted to Arthur Herbert Tennyson Somers Cocks (d. 1944), sixth Baron Somers, and to his daughter Elizabeth (d. 1986), who married Benjamin Hervey-Bathurst. In 2012 their sons, James and George Hervey-Bathurst, held it through shareholdings in Eastnor Castle Estate Company, established in 1940.[79]

74   HRO, CD78/1: baptismal register s.a. 1820.
75   Eastnor Castle Mun., Ledger 1890–6, pp. 1, 3.
76   *Domesday Book, Herefordshire* (Phillimore 1983), 2,27 (f. 182).
77   Eastnor Castle Mun., Eastnor Parish box 2; ibid., case 1, bundle 9.
78   *VCH Surrey*, iii, Reigate, Manors, www.british-history.ac.uk/report.aspx?compid=42960&strquery=Reig ate#s4, accessed 17 January 2012.
79   *Complete Peerage*, ix (1), s.v. Somers of Evesham; *Eastnor Castle Guide* (2003 edn.); inf. from Mr James Hervey-Bathurst.

The bishop's manor house stood on the site of the modern Eastnor Farm, the home farm of the Eastnor estate. In 1404 the house, with its garden and other land around it, was worth nothing.[80] In 1496 the bishop leased the 'farmplace' of the manor to the yeoman Henry Branch for 40 years.[81] In 1578 the site of the manor, formerly held by John Branch, was held by the assigns of Richard Delabere, who had obtained a 60-year lease from the bishop in 1551.[82] In 1743 the lease was acquired by an Eastnor yeoman, Benjamin Burrop, who renewed it in 1764.[83] In 1772 the farmhouse, still in the occupation of Benjamin Burrop, passed by exchange to Charles Cocks of Castleditch.[84]

In 1086 two unnamed subtenants, a knight and a mason, held a ½ hide and a ½ hide with ½ yardland respectively of the bishop's Eastnor manor.[85] By c. 1288 those two holdings had become two tenancies in return for which military service was required: 2 yardlands were held by William de Homme, and 4 yardlands held by William de Gateley. William de Homme held a further yardland and William de Gateley a further 2½ yardlands in socage.[86]

Castleditch (sub-manor)

The estate, called a manor in 1385,[87] derived from William de Homme's freehold, which passed, probably before c. 1340, to the Clintons, who enlarged their estate over the next 150–200 years. Ivo de Clinton was active in Eastnor or its neighbourhood between 1337 and 1347; he died before 1360.[88] In 1385 John Clinton, presumably Ivo's heir, had the bishop of Hereford's licence to have mass celebrated at Castleditch.[89] He witnessed several Eastnor deeds between 1389 and 1415.[90] The next certainly known member of the family, Robert Clinton, was recorded between 1421 and 1445.[91] He was probably preceded by another Ivo Clinton, for a note among the records of St Katherine's hospital recorded that land held from the hospital by Robert Clinton had previously been held by Agnes de Clinton, then her son John, and then John's son Ivo, before Robert.[92] In 1469 the manor was held by another John Clinton,[93] probably the John Clinton who died in 1502 or 1503

80   *Cal. Inq. Misc.* vii (1339–1422), no. 281, p. 152.
81   *Cat. Anc. D.* vi, C. 7162.
82   HRO, B049 (microfilm of Longleat House MS41); ibid., AA59 A2, f. 94v.
83   Eastnor Castle Mun., case 4, bundle 5.
84   ibid., case 1, bundle 6. For a description of the building, see above, Domestic Buildings.
85   *Domesday Book, Herefordshire*, 2, 27 (f. 182).
86   HRO, AA59 A1, p. 143.
87   *Reg. Gilbert*, 94.
88   DCA 7018/2, f. 11v.–12; BL Add Ch 72732: reference kindly supplied by John Freeman from EPNS notes; HRO, CF50/178, Heref DD 19 (Cal of BL Add Ch 72733); Heref H 70 (BL Add Ch 72744).
89   *Reg. Gilbert*, 94.
90   HRO, CF50/178, Heref II 27 (Cal of BL Add Ch 72793); Heref II 31 (BL Add Ch 72798); Heref G 22 (BL Add Ch 72801); Heref G 26 (BL Add Ch 72804); Heref G 65 (BL Add Ch 72814); Heref G 72 (BL Add Ch 72816); Heref FF 31 (BL Add Ch 72819); BL AddCh, 72811: reference supplied by John Freeman from EPNS notes.
91   HRO, CF50/178 Heref GG 10 (Cal of BL Add Ch 72827); Heref DD 5 (BL Add Ch 72840); *Cal. Fine R.* xvi (1430–7), 235; *Cal. Pat.* 1441–6, 406.
92   DCA 7018/2, p. 89.
93   *Cal. Close* Edw IV, vol. 2, no. 459.

leaving his elder son William to inherit most of his possessions.[94] William died in 1534, holding the manors of Castleditch and Goodings, the latter being the second medieval freehold in the parish; he made provision in his will for prayers for the souls of Robert, John, and William Clinton, presumably himself, his father, and his grandfather. His son Thomas Clinton died in 1575, and was succeeded by his son Francis.[95]

In 1578 Francis Clinton held Castleditch and 2 yardlands as ⅛ of a knight's fee, in addition to several other free and copyhold houses and lands.[96] He was last recorded in 1582, and in 1591 his son Ivo attended the bishop of Hereford's Eastnor court.[97] By 1605 Ivo was in financial difficulties and trying to arrange a mortgage. That year or the next Castleditch passed, probably by sale, to Richard Cocks, who was a London grocer and an associate of some of Clinton's London contacts, and whose family came from Bishop's Cleeve (Glos.). Richard died in 1623 and was succeeded by his son, Thomas.[98] Thomas (d. 1649) was succeeded by his son, another Thomas (d. 1705), and then by that Thomas's sons, John (d. 1718) and Thomas (d. 1724), successively.[99] From the last Thomas the manor passed to his daughter Mary and to her husband, her cousin John Cocks; John was the nephew of John Somers, first Baron Somers, who had been Lord Chancellor from 1697 to 1700.[100] John Cocks died in 1771 and was succeeded by his and Mary's son, Charles,[101] who in 1772 assumed the baronetcy of Cocks of Dumbleton, (Glos.), and in 1784 was created Baron Somers of Evesham, the barony first created in 1697 for his great uncle, John Somers.[102] In 1785 Charles acquired the manor of Eastnor from the bishop of Hereford by exchanging it, and thereafter Castleditch descended with that manor, (that is, both manors were inherited by the same lords).

Goodings or Old Court (sub-manor)

The names of William de Gateley, John de Gately, and another William de Gately occur in Eastnor charters between the mid 12th and the mid 13th centuries.[103] About 1288 William de Gateley, perhaps a third man of the name, held 4 yardlands in Eastnor of the bishop by knight service, and a further 2½ yardlands in socage (payment of a non-military obligation, usually rent).[104] He or another William de Gateley held the estate of the bishop in 1304, but there is no further record of the family at Eastnor, and their lands

94 TNA, PROB 11/13, will of John Clynton.
95 Eastnor Castle Mun., Castleditch box, rental of Thomas Clinton 1552, fragment of notes from rentals; *Cal. Hereford Probate Acts*, ed. M.A. Faraday (2008), pp. 268, 386; TNA, C 142/82/54; ibid. PROB 11/58: will of Thomas Clynton; HRO, MX334 (microfilm of Eastnor par. Reg.), 23 December 1575.
96 HRO, AA59 A2, ff. 95, 97.
97 ibid., AM33/7; Eastnor Castle Mun., case 2, bundle 1A.
98 Eastnor Castle Mun., Castleditch box; *Little Malvern Letters*, i, (Catholic Record Soc. 83, 2011), 89, 91; MI (copied in Herefs. Family Hist. Soc. 'Monumental Inscriptions Survey: Eastnor', p. 35).
99 For the Cocks family descent, see H. L. Somers-Cocks, *Eastnor and its Malvern Hills* (1923), 115–38.
100 *Complete Peerage*, ix (1), s.v. Somers of Evesham.
101 Eastnor Castle Mun., case 1, bundle 5.
102 *Complete Peerage*, ix (1), s.v. Somers of Evesham.
103 HRO, AH82/3; DCA, 3667, 3684.
104 HRO, AA59 A1, p. 143.

passed to the Delaberes, a Herefordshire gentry family.[105] Sir John Delabere held land in Eastnor in 1349 and 1360.[106] Sir Kynard Delabere of Kinnersley held that estate by 1391; at his death in 1400 or 1401 he was succeeded by his son, Richard.[107] He or another Richard Delabere held it in 1437, 1467, and 1477.[108] Sir Richard Delabere of Kinnersley, probably a third man of the name, held in 1506 and died in 1514 holding what was described as 'the manor of Eastnor'; his son and heir, Thomas, died in 1518 or 1519.[109] By 1534 Thomas's heirs had conveyed the manor, then called Goodings, to William Clinton of Castleditch.[110]

Bronsil Manor

The manor derives from lands obtained piecemeal by John, Lord Beauchamp of Powick, and his son, Richard, in the mid 15th century.[111] Among them was land at Deerfold and Horton which had been given to Little Malvern priory in the early 13th century.[112] In 1460 Richard Beauchamp had licence to build and crenellate (fortify) a 'tower' on land he was emparking in Eastnor.[113] The land appears to have been held directly from the Crown, not from the bishop of Hereford. In 1470, when it was settled on John Beauchamp and his heirs, the estate was described as the manor and 'town' of Bronsil.[114] The attraction of Eastnor was probably the hunting: by 1497 Richard Beauchamp was forester of Malvern Chase.[115] In 1500 he conveyed Bronsil to Sir Gilbert Talbot, who granted it back to him to hold for his life.[116] Richard died in 1503,[117] and Bronsil presumably passed to Gilbert Talbot, who dealt with land in Eastnor in 1506.[118]

By 1544 Bronsil was in the possession of Sir John Talbot, who that year granted an 80-year lease of most of the estate to George Alyngton of Hanbury (Worcs.), although he retained the right to stay at the castle whenever he wished.[119] In 1569 Sir John's son, Gilbert Talbot, conveyed the castle and lordship to John Talbot of Grafton (Worcs.),

105 *Reg. Ric. Swinfield*, ii. 403; HRO, AA59 A1, p. 143 (marginal note).
106 DCA 7018, f. 12; HRO, CF50/178, Heref H 91 (Cal of BL Add Ch 72747).
107 HRO, CF50/178, Heref G 3 (Cal of BL Add Ch 72800); TNA, PROB 11/2A: will of Kynard Delabere.
108 HRO, CF50/178, Heref BB 1 (Cal of BL Add Ch 72842); Heref A 28 (BL Add MS 46458 f.6); Heref. L 27 (BL Add Ch. 72878).
109 HRO, CF50/178, Heref Y 9 (Cal of BL Add MS 46458, f. 26); TNA, C 142/29/43; C 142/33/17.
110 TNA, C 142/82/54.
111 HRO, AH82/16; *Cal. Close. 1468–76, 459*; Hist. MSS Com. 55, *MSS in Various Collections* (1903) [Cd 932], 295. On John Beauchamp (1400–75), a distinguished royal servant and treasurer 1450–2, see *Oxford DNB*.
112 HRO, AH82/2; Hist. MSS Com. 55, *MSS in Various Collections*, 295.
113 *Cal. Chart. R.* vi. (1427–1516), 137.
114 *Cal. Close. 1468–76*, 459, vol. 2, no. 459, www.british-history.ac.uk, accessed 19 November 2009; TNA, CP 25/1/83/57, no. 9, www.medievalgenealogy.org.uk/fines/abstracts/, accessed 8 January 2010.
115 HRO, AM33/12.
116 ibid., CF50/178, Heref J 34 (Cal. of BL Add Ch 72894); Hist. MSS Com. 55, *MSS in Various Collections*, 302.
117 *Complete Peerage*, ii. 47.
118 TNA, CP 25/1/83/58, no. 24, www.medievalgenealogy.org.uk/fines/abstracts/, accessed 8 January 2010.
119 Eastnor Castle Mun., Bronsil box.

ancestor of the earls of Shrewsbury.[120] Later that year John conveyed the castle and land, subject to an annual rent charge, to William and Mary Reed of Boddington (Glos.).[121] In 1633 John Talbot, earl of Shrewsbury, conveyed the rent charge to their descendant, William Reed of Lugwardine (d. 1634).[122] Bronsil descended in the Reed family to Thomas Reed (d. 1743), and to his daughter Mary and her husband, Dormer Sheldon (d. 1772). Their son Thomas sold Bronsil to Charles Cocks of Castleditch in 1774.[123]

Bronsil Castle

The Talbot charters, which record in detail John and Richard Beauchamp's acquisition of the Bronsil estate, do not refer to any earlier house, so the castle was almost certainly the first building on the site. Like other later medieval castles such as Bodiam (Sussex) and Treago in St Weonards, Bronsil was built to display its owner's status, and its plan and setting have been compared to the contemporary 'pleasaunce' or pleasure house and garden at Kenilworth Castle (Warws.).[124] The almost square castle probably stood within a double moat. It was surrounded by curtain walls which had towers at all corners

Figure 4 *Bronsil Castle as drawn by Samuel and Nathaniel Buck in 1731. Probably a fanciful view, though its ruinous state on a moated site at the foot of the Malvern Hills reflects the truth.*

120 BL Add Ch 72906: reference supplied by John Freeman from EPNS notes; *Complete Peerage*, xi., 706n.
121 Eastnor Castle Mun., Bronsil box; HRO, AA59 A2, f. 95v.; Somers-Cocks, *Eastnor and its Malvern Hills*, 156–7.
122 *Trans. Bristol and Glos. Arch. Soc.* lx (1938), 280; Eastnor Castle Mun., Castleditch box; C.J. Robinson, *Mansions and Manors of Herefordshire* (1873, reprinted Logaston Press, 2001), 190.
123 Eastnor Castle Mun., case 1, bundle 5; case 4, bundle 1; Bronsil box; HRO, CF50/96, p. 346. For Dormer Sheldon, rector of Shenington (Oxon. formerly Glos.) see *VCH Oxon.* ix. 148.
124 Brooks and Pevsner, *Herefordshire* (2012), 222, 591; www. herefordshire.gov.uk/smrSearch/Monuments/ Monument_Item.aspx?ID=934, accessed 26 May 2013.

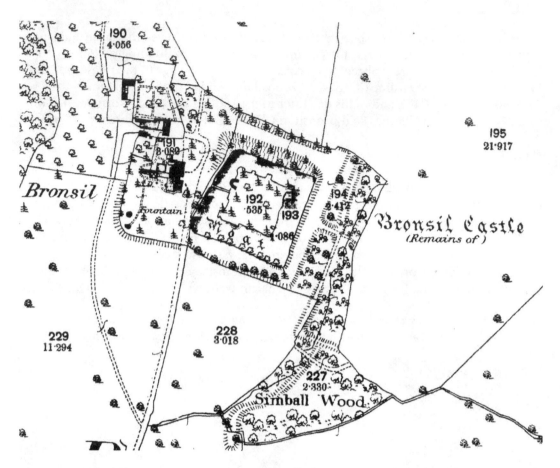

Map 5   *The moated remains of Bronsil Castle, with Bronsil House to its west in 1892.*

but the south-east, with intermediate towers in the north, south and east walls. In the west wall was the gatehouse, flanked by two further towers. There is no archaeological evidence for the buildings within the curtain wall, but the lease of 1544 referred to the dining chamber at the end of the winding stair and the chambers at the upper end of the little stair.[125] The castle appears to have been occupied by the Reeds in the later 16th and the early 17th centuries, as members of the family were baptised in Eastnor between 1567 and 1617, but there is no clear evidence for the family there after 1617, and in 1633 William Reed was described as of Newcourt, Lugwardine.[126] In 1709 the castle was uninhabitable, having been largely demolished during the Civil War; it had been replaced by a house deemed unsuitable as a residence for the lord of the manor.[127]

Parts of the towers and curtain walls survived in 1731 when the castle was drawn, probably not altogether accurately, by Samuel and Nathaniel Buck, but by 1779 only one tower remained. The site was cleared and tidied and a new bridge built across the moat *c.* 1840, probably as part of the renovation and improvement of Bronsil Cottage which

125 Eastnor Castle Mun., Bronsil box.
126 *Trans Bristol and Glos. Arch. Soc.* lx (1938), 280.
127 TNA, C 6/91/139.

stands across the moat on the west. Most of the surviving tower, a gate tower, collapsed into the moat in 1990. In 2012 only small parts of the gate tower and of a newel staircase and fragments of three walls, as well as the earthworks of the moat and associated ponds, survived.[128]

Massington Estate, later Manor

In 1242 Walter de Eyneford claimed that Bishop Ralph of Maidstone (bishop of Hereford 1234–9) had granted him a ploughland (about 120 a.) in Massington.[129] The bishop's rental of *c.* 1288 records that the heirs of Alan of Wellington held 1½ hides in Wellington and Massington, and John Massington held 2 yardlands in Ledbury parish, perhaps in Massington; both estates were held by knight service.[130] Massington was called a manor in 1401, when land there was held of Agnes, widow of Hugh Carew the younger, presumably lady of the manor.[131] At his death in 1415 Thomas Walwyn of Much Marcle left land in Massington to his younger son Malcolm.[132] Malcolm Walwyn, presumably another man of the same name, held Massington of the bishop's Eastnor manor in 1467.[133] In 1524, when an assessment was made for taxation, Richard Monyngton was by far the wealthiest man in the vill and presumably already lord of the manor.[134] About the early 1540s he sold Massington manor to Rowland and Sybil Morton of Twining (Glos.).[135] Richard Cocks of Castleditch held Massington at his death in 1624.[136]

Massington Farm

The house incorporates in its north-east wing part of a 15th-century, box-framed open hall, into which a floor has been inserted. The main part of the half-H-plan house is of the 17th century, built of rubble and brick.[137]

The St Katherine's Hospital Estate

In the 50 years or so after its foundation *c.* 1230 St Katherine's Hospital, Ledbury, acquired a considerable estate in Eastnor and the adjoining part of Ledbury parish later

128 R. Shoesmith, *Castles and Moated Sites of Herefordshire* (Logaston Press, 2nd edn 2009), 111–18; NMR, English Heritage, Survey Report on Bronsil Castle (2000).
129 *Cur. Reg. R.* xvi, no. 2013, p. 411.
130 HRO, AA59/A/1, p. 133.
131 TNA, C 143/431/3.
132 ibid., PROB 11/2B, will of Thomas Walwyn.
133 HRO, CF50/178, Heref A 28 (Cal of BL Add MS 46458 f.6).
134 M.A. Faraday, *Herefordshire taxes in the reign of Henry VIII* (Woolhope Club, Hereford, 2005), 71.
135 TNA, C 1/1145/72.
136 Eastnor Castle Mun., Cox box 1.
137 RCHME, *Herefordshire*, ii. 41; J. Tonkin, 'Medieval Houses of Herefordshire', *Herefordshire Miscellany*, ed. D. Whitehead and J. Eisel (Woolhope Club, 2000), 79.

called Netherton.[138] The hospital and its endowments survived the Dissolution,[139] but by the late 16th century it was hard to identify some of the lands, which hospital rentals and other documents show were in the hands of tenants including Francis Clinton and his successor Richard Cocks.[140] In 1612 the hospital leased its Netherton estate to John Bridges of Ockeridge, a neighbouring farm. The lease, renewed in 1783, had come into the hands of Charles Cocks, Baron Somers, by 1785 when he had a copy made of a terrier (description) of the estate.[141] In 1804 and 1805 Lord Somers leased a total of 61 a. of the hospital's land. Negotiations for the sale of the whole estate to Lord Somers seem to have started in 1805, but problems arose because it was almost impossible to prove where exactly the hospital lands lay. In 1812 the hospital finally exchanged its Eastnor lands, agreed to total *c.* 119 a., with Earl Somers for land in Thornbury.[142]

LOCAL GOVERNMENT

In the Middle Ages Eastnor was governed through local courts, principally those of the bishop of Hereford as lord of Eastnor manor and of the Clintons as lords of Castleditch. Within the wider county administration, Eastnor formed part of Radlow hundred, the hundreds being subdivisions of the county which had their own courts and officers. The court for Radlow hundred met in Ledbury, its market town, but no records of its proceedings survive.[143] The courts were responsible for some aspects of criminal justice, for maintaining peace, and for controlling standards in the market. Peace was maintained by a system of 'tithings', that is groups, originally of ten men, who were responsible for each other's conduct. All men over twelve years old had to be enrolled into a tithing and the system was overseen by special courts called views of frankpledge. The sale of bread and ale was controlled by the assizes of bread and of ale, statutory regulations as to the price and quality of those two staple foods. Not all manorial courts had the right to this extensive jurisdiction, but in the late 13th century the bishop of Hereford successfully claimed it in all his manors, including Eastnor. The hundred was also the unit for local taxation, the taxes, known as subsidies, being assessed and collected by local landowners. In 1546 and 1547 Thomas Clinton of Castleditch was high collector for Radlow hundred.[144]

Manorial Courts

The bishop of Hereford held courts for his manors at Hereford and at Ledbury, and the free tenants in Eastnor owed suit to (that is were obliged to attend) both courts.

138 J. Hillaby, *St Katherine's Hospital Ledbury c. 1230–1547* (Logaston Press, 2003), 45–7. Many of the original charters are in Hereford Cathedral Library, DCA.
139 S. Pinches, *Ledbury, a market town and its Tudor heritage*, 79–80.
140 DCA 3582, 3766.
141 Eastnor Castle Mun., Case 4; DCA 3600.
142 DCA 3600, 3766.
143 S. Pinches, *Ledbury; people and parish before the Reformation* (2010), 73–4.
144 *Herefordshire Taxes in the Reign of Henry VIII*, ed. M.A. Faraday (Woolhope Club, 2005), 27.

Other tenants presumably attended only the bishop's Eastnor court. A surviving mid 13th-century deed may well have been made in that court, since it was witnessed by the bishop's seneschal together with his bailiff and six leading Eastnor landholders.[145] No medieval court records survive for Eastnor, although the profits (5s. and 32s. 8d.) from fines levied were entered into the manorial accounts in 1404 and 1497, and only three 16th-century ones remain, for courts in 1555, 1556 and 1591.[146] Proceedings in 1555 included two cases of fighting or 'affray', a complaint of an unscoured ditch between the rector's land and that of William Weobley, and a report of two unclaimed stray sheep; in 1556 William Challoner was accused of breaking a hedge, perhaps in a dispute over an inclosure. In 1591 three ale-house keepers were accused of breaking the assize of bread and ale, and two men of diverting a stream; the court decreed that no cottager should cut down trees without permission; the rest of the court business was to record transfers of copyhold land. Later courts seem to have been concerned only with land transactions. They were still being held for that purpose in 1783, and probably as late as 1804, by which time the manor had passed to Lord Somers.[147]

The Cocks family held courts for their manors of Castleditch and Goodings or Old Court, both sub-manors of the bishop's manor. The main business of the two courts for which records survive, in 1630 and 1631, was the renewal of the manorial rental, a list of tenants and their rents, but the court also fined ten tenants for failing to attend the court and accused one man of digging up and carrying away soil from a field. A court in 1638 dealt only with transfers of land.[148]

St Katherine's Hospital held courts for all its manors from the 14th century or earlier, although no records of the Ledbury court, whose jurisdiction covered Eastnor, survive before 1516. That court seems to have been concerned solely with land tenure, but earlier courts for Kempley and Weston fined tenants for knocking down a hedge and for brewing, presumably in breach of the assize of ale.[149] The Ledbury courts would have exercised a similar jurisdiction.

In 1413 or 1414 a dispute over a house and land, later part of the Bronsil estate, was settled by four arbiters meeting in Eastnor church,[150] but the meeting was not described as a court. In the early 19th century there was no knowledge or record of any courts for Bronsil or Massington, and there was no copyhold land on either manor.[151]

145 HRO, AH82/7.
146 *Cal. Inq. Misc.* vii (1339–1422), no. 281, p. 152; HRO, AM33/4, AM33/12.
147 Eastnor Castle Mun., case 2, bundle 6; case 3, bundle 1; case 4, bundles 1, 5, 31.
148 ibid., Castleditch box; ibid., case 4, bundle. 1: 17th-century manor court documents for manor of Goodyngs or Old Court.
149 DCA 7018/2, pp. 45, 72v., 91. This MS contains notes only, not the complete rolls.
150 Hist. MSS Com. 55, *MSS in Various Collections* (1903) [Cd 932], 295.
151 HRO, CF50/96.

Parochial Government

From the 16th century onwards the churchwardens and other parish officers, notably
the overseers of the poor, played an increasingly important part in local government;
their meetings were known as the vestry (from the room in which they were held). The
Eastnor churchwardens were recorded in 1652 when, with the minister of the parish,
they were placed in charge of a charity established by Thomas Danford's will,[152] but the
office had certainly been in existence long before then. There are, however, no records of
vestry government for Eastnor: the few later 19th-century vestry meetings recorded in
the churchwardens' book dealt solely with church affairs.[153]

Eastnor was in Ledbury Poor Law Union from 1834, and the Ledbury Rural District
from 1894 to 1974.[154] When Herefordshire and Worcestershire were united under the
local government reorganisation of 1974, Eastnor became part of the Malvern Hills
District. In 1998 the parish became part of Ledbury Ward in the Herefordshire Unitary
Authority.

152 TNA, PROB 11/238, will of Thomas Danford the elder.
153 HRO, CD78/62.
154 F. Youngs, *Local Administrative Units, Northern England* (Royal Hist. Soc., 1991), 671; www.
     visionofbritain.org.uk/relationships.jsp?u_id=10068046&c_id=10001043, accessed 24 January 2012.

The Predecessor of the Castle, Castleditch House

THE MANOR HOUSE OF Castleditch stood near the site of the 19th-century Eastnor Castle, by 1385.[1] In 1624 the ground-floor rooms included the hall, great parlour and little parlour with an adjoining entry and little buttery; the house was taxed on 12 hearths in 1665.[2] The moated house shown by the Glynch brook east of the site of the later castle on a map of 1726 may have started as a hall with cross-wing; it seems to have been extended eastwards at different times, creating a rectangular building entered on the south side and perhaps with a central courtyard and a central cupola. West and south of the house were ancillary buildings, including a dovecote, on the southern slope were terraced walks, and a fish pool lay on the brook.

By the 1790s, the old house with jettied cross-wing had been disguised by stucco and a classical centrepiece added to the entrance front. A new eastern block, with two full-height semi-circular bows overlooking the pleasure grounds, had been built *c.* 1780 for Charles Cocks, first Baron Somers of Evesham; the designer was probably the Gloucestershire architect Anthony Keck, a protégé of Dr Treadway Nash, father-in-law to the baron's son.[3] What had been described as 'a small plain building in white stone…built on a modern plan,'[4] was demolished in 1814 as the rising water of the new lake reduced its site to an island. Its materials were reused in Eastnor Castle.[5]

Eastnor Castle

The castle was designed for John Somers Cocks, first Earl and second Baron Somers (d. 1852), by Robert Smirke in his 'new square style', a departure from the Gothic manner he had employed at Lowther Castle (Westmoreland) for Lord Londsdale. The foundation stone was laid in April 1812. Rising costs during construction resulted in the castle being left incomplete and without stables for many years.[6] The accounts suggest

1   *Reg. Gilbert*, 94. The following chapter on Castleditch and Eastnor Castle was written by David Whitehead. For Castleditch manor *see* Introduction, Landownership.
2   Eastnor Castle Mun., Cox box 1, fragment of inventory of Richard Cocks, printed in Somers Cocks, *Eastnor and Its Malvern Hills*, 121; HRO Libr., TS copy of Hearth Tax, by J. Harnden.
3   *Oxford DNB*, 'Keck, Anthony (1726/7–1797)'; G. Beard, 'Nash: Historian of Worcestershire', *Trans. Worcs. Archaeol. Soc.* xxxii (1956), 14–22.
4   J. Chambers, *A General History of Malvern* (1817), 229.
5   Eastnor Castle Mun., Smirke Accounts 6 (1814).
6   Eastnor Castle Mun., Smirke letter *c.* 1811, undated but annotated by the first Earl Somers.

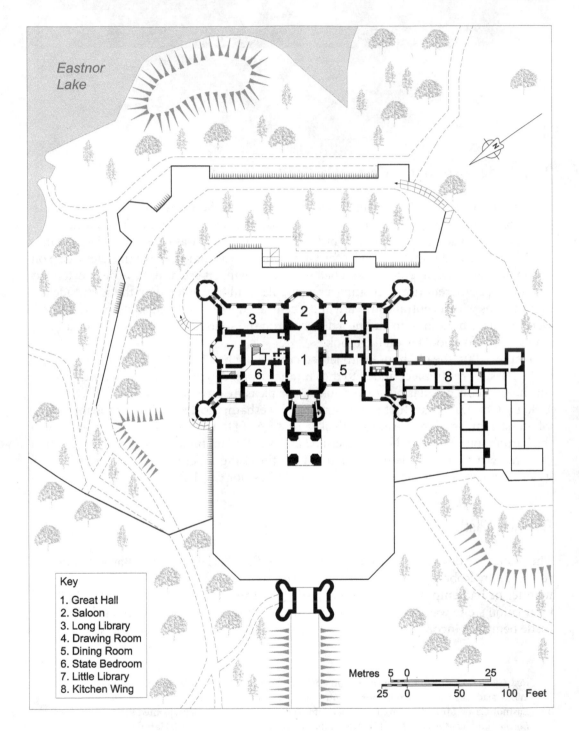

Eastnor
Lake

Key

1. Great Hall
2. Saloon
3. Long Library
4. Drawing Room
5. Dining Room
6. State Bedroom
7. Little Library
8. Kitchen Wing

Metres 5   0   25

25   0   50   100 Feet

Figure 5 *Eastnor Castle, showing its raised, terraced site and its principal ground-floor rooms.*

that the total cost was *c*. £90,000 but contemporary and modern estimates have put the figure much higher.[7]

Smirke's design was Norman rather than Gothic, the large areas of plain ashlar and round-headed windows contributing to an impression of massiveness.[8] In plan, the castle is rectangular and has at each angle, attached by a slender corridor, a tall clover-leaf tower, originally designed to carry a turret. The main north–south axis is filled with a great hall, entered through a carriage porch, and an octagonal saloon, both of which rise to three storeys. They were designed to impress, with a *route d' honneur* stepping up through the entrance hall into the great hall and reaching a climax in the octagonal saloon, which afforded spectacular views across the lake and towards the Malvern Hills and family obelisk, built in 1811.[9] The great hall was the centrepiece of the design, where the Romanesque theme was reinforced with a first-floor blind arcade and a glazed clerestory. The octagon saloon linked the drawing room and the long library to form a suite of important reception rooms along the south front.[10]

Building the Castle

Ashlar was brought at considerable expense from the Forest of Dean (Glos.), using the new tramways and port facilities at Lydney and Bullo Pill in which Lord Somers seems to have had a financial interest.[11] Local limestone was used for the foundations, inner walls, and the service wing. A quarry was opened (it survives near the north drive) and a temporary tram-road was constructed to deliver the stone to all parts of the building as required. The plates, pins, and stubs were supplied by William Montague of the Bradley Forge, Forest of Dean.

The corner towers went up in 1812 and the roof followed the next year.[12] Eighteen cast-iron beams, to form roof trusses and floor and ceiling joists, and 58 wall plates, altogether weighing 16 tons, were delivered to Upton-on-Severn (Worcs.). From there they were dragged by horse and cart over the Malvern Hills, with labourers repairing the public road as the cavalcade progressed.[13] Smirke, one of the first British architects to use load-bearing cast iron in domestic architecture, later stated that he adopted iron at Eastnor because Baltic timber had become scarce and expensive as a result of Napoleon's Continental blockade.[14] In some parts of the roof even the laths for taking the slates were made of iron, and an engineer, Samuel Bowden, was sent from Stockport (Ches.) to supervise use of the relatively untried material.[15]

7   G. Beard, *Craftsmen and Interior Decoration in England 1660-1820* (1981), 227-31.

8   Brooks and Pevsner, *Herefordshire* (2012), 219–22.

9   Eastnor Castle Mun., Smirke plans. There are over 200 working drawings.

10   Below, Interior Decoration.

11   *VCH Gloucestershire* V (1996), 350–2.

12   Eastnor Castle Mun., Smirke Accounts, 1–2; Smirke's perspective drawings are framed and hung in the castle.

13   Eastnor Castle Mun., Smirke Accounts, 3, f.15.

14   ibid., letter from Thomas Foley *c*. 1950 quoting a newspaper cutting.

15   Smirke's methods of construction with cast iron at Eastnor may have formed a prototype for his use of it elsewhere.

Figure 6 *Castleditch house, showing the south front much as it looked in 1726 (Fig. 13), and the eastern range added c. 1800.*

Figure 7 *Eastnor Castle from the lake, raised on its artificial terraces. The medieval architectural style is evocative rather than archaeologically correct in every detail.*

Smirke employed several other technical innovations. A mortar mill, with two grind stones, was built of iron and wood by a local smith, and a horse-driven pug mill, to mix the clay and sand for the bricks, seems to have been introduced by the mason, George Wood. A hoist for lifting stone, made of large timbers called 'shears', was apparently superseded in March 1814 when Smirke informed Lord Somers that he had bought a 'hydraulic machine', reduced in price from £150 to £70.

Plumbing

Among the convenient modern devices provided in 1814 was a 'brass water engine', part of the 'apparatus for water-closets' that included a 'brass open-headed pan with a wrought handle and brass hinges'. A specialist plumber travelled from London to give advice on fitting. The 'apparatus' had a 16 in. drain trap, connected via a larger service pipe to a cess-pool in a remote area of the garden.[16]

One of the principal endeavours was to bring piped water to the Castle. A pipe was laid from a spring close to the church, which delivered water to a tank beneath the outer gatehouse where a water engine was to be built beside it. Plans had been drawn up by Smirke as early as May 1815, but the engine was not delivered until June 1816; in September Lord Somers was urging his architect to put men on the job and in 1817 work was in progress. A little later, a millwright was 'fixing a water-engine for the Castle', probably the 'forcing pump' provided by the Boulton and Watt company.[17]

Interior decoration

In December 1813 the London craftsmen Francis Bernasconi, plasterer, assisted by Cornelius Dixon, decorator, began enriching the interior,[18] but the work was left in a relatively unfinished state in 1819, when the earl found he could not afford to continue it.[19] Completion was delayed until the mid 19th century, after the accession of the second earl in 1841. A reference in October 1849 to 'the new rooms ... boarded and ready for use' suggests that the earl was considering redecorating one or more of the principal rooms.[20] He would have been familiar with the redecoration of the House of Lords chamber, completed in 1847. Its decorator, J.G. Crace, produced a scheme for the Eastnor drawing room,[21] consulting A.W.N. Pugin whose role was probably peripheral.[22] Pugin designed a chimneypiece, with copious references to the Somers family, but it was too substantial for the castle's comparatively flimsy walls, and Lord Somers noted in November 1849 that he had been persuaded to have it 'brought forward' into the room, relying upon the contractor and Crace to use their skill to disguise the inconvenience.

16   Eastnor Castle Mun., Smirke Accounts, 6 ff.59-60.
17   ibid., Smirke Accounts, 8, f.20; 10, f.17; 12, f.9, 11v; 14, ff.4–5.
18   For Bernasconi and Dixon see Beard, *Craftsmen and Interior Decoration*, 246–7, 256.
19   *Complete Diary of a Cotswold Parson: diaries of Revd Francis Edward Witts 1783–1854*, ed. A. Sutton (2008), iii. 435–7. He had heard that the final cost of building the castle was close to £200,000.
20   Eastnor Castle Mun., third Earl's correspondence, box 2: Harriet Cocks to her brother Charles, later the third Earl.
21   ibid., second Earl's diary, box 1, 6 Nov. 1849.
22   R. Hill, *God's Architect* (2007), 248.

On 30 August 1850 Pugin made his only visit to inspect the work and, the day after, Lord Somers paid Messrs Crace £500.[23] Writing to her mother, the countess, Lady Harriet Somers Cocks described how 'everyone admires the room excessively ... the fame of it has spread far and wide and at Malvern the report is that the Queen is coming'.[24]

In 1852 George McCann, perhaps under the guidance of Sir George Gilbert Scott,[25] began to create a new suite of rooms for the third earl, Charles Somers Cocks, who had inherited the estate that year. Work started with the refenestration of the great hall but plans, including those for a new gothic ceiling designed by Scott,[26] were put on hold in 1853 when a visit to Italy with Henry Layard (1817-94), the explorer and diplomat, resulted in Lord Somers's taste being converted from Gothic to Italian Renaissance style.[27] McCann received the final payment in November 1855. Subsequently materials for the completion of the hall were collected, including stone, alabaster and marble, and a new contractor, Thomas Collins of Tewkesbury, was engaged.

Figure 8 *The Drawing Room c. 1910, as decorated in Gothic style by J.G. Crace who incorporated the chimneypiece designed by A.W.N. Pugin.*

23   Eastnor Castle Mun., second Earl's diary, box 1, 29 Nov. 1849; box 2, bank book for 1850.
24   ibid., third Earl's correspondence, box 2.
25   Below, Religious Life, St John's church.
26   Eastnor Castle Mun., General Accounts 4, Sept. 1852–April 1854. There is an undated drawing for the new Great Hall, endorsed by George Gilbert Scott, among the Smirke plans.
27   Eastnor Castle Mun., third Earl, box 2 – a letter with attachments from Dorothy Simmons.

In March 1860 the third earl met the painter and muralist G.E. Fox and the sculptor William Forsyth of Worcester at Eastnor to discuss his new ideas for the great hall,[28] and in October Fox visited churches in Poitou (France) 'to take in ideas for the Hall'. Between 1862 and 1864 its Romanesque character was reinforced, the inspiration being the Norman architecture of the Mediterranean rather than that of Northern Europe. Forsyth enriched Smirke's blind arcade with marble columns, turned and polished by a London craftsman, William Field. The alabaster capitals were copied from casts of models in the South Kensington (V&A) museum, and the same casts were used on a larger scale for columns flanking the hall's main entrances. Fox painted repetitive 'Saracenic' designs on canvas attached to the walls below the arcade. Smirke's timber roof was cleaned and left with a natural finish.[29]

In 1862 financial difficulties led the third earl to threaten to stop all expenditure, apart from supporting Fox, who accompanied him to Italy on a sketching expedition 'to make some studies'. The following year Fox supervised work in the long and little libraries, the octagon saloon, and in the large dining room where he painted coats of arms against a blue background within each panel of Smirke's ceiling.[30] Other rooms on the east front were given oak sashes with plate glass and new decoration. The work was carried out over the next decade by Lord Somers and Layard with fastidious connoisseurship.[31] In the long library, inlaid bookcases, designed by Fox, were made by Farenza, a Venetian craftsman whose workshop Lord Somers inspected in April 1868. The chimney pieces were worked up in Istrian marble by the Veronese sculptor Pegrassi from casts, which had been obtained from the Doge's Palace, Venice, by the historian Rawdon Brown (1803–83) and which arrived at Eastnor in December 1866. By then Fox had completed the emblematic ceiling with figures in Quattrocento style.[32] The ceiling of the octagon saloon had to be strengthened with an iron truss to take the weight of a chandelier. From 1863 to 1869 the estate carpenters regularly erected on site 'models' for the ceiling and for the chimney piece by Forsyth.[33] Coloured presentation sketches, one dated 14 June 1869, were made for the ceiling, depicting sea-gods, satyrs and grotesque decoration, their Mediterranean character intended to echo the scene beyond the garden doors. The paintings were never executed and in November 1869 Lord Somers found

28   ibid., General Accounts 4; Letters to Virginia, third Countess, 20 Aug. 1860. Fox, painter and muralist, appears to have been a protégé of the artist G.F. Watts (1817–1904), member of a group around the earl's sister-in-law, Sara Prinsep; see V.F. Gould, *G.F. Watts: The Last Great Victorian* (2004), *passim*. For Fox's work see *Country Life*, 28 Nov. 2012. For Forsyth H.G. Gwilliam, *Old Worcester* II (1977), 54; Brooks and Pevsner, *Worcestershire* (2007), 328, and *passim*.

29   Eastnor Castle Mun., General Accounts 1860–4; ibid., Letters to Virginia 1860–4.

30   ibid., Letters to Virginia, 6 Dec. 1860, 21 Oct. 1860, 1 November 1860, undated Nov. 1862.

31   ibid., Dining Room-2/3 Nov. 1870; General Accounts 5–6 for regular work on the windows between 1860 and 1863; Leyard's contribution has been summarised by Dorothy Simmons, see third Earl's box 2.

32   Eastnor Castle Mun., Letters to Virginia, undated Nov. 1862–1873; letters to the third Earl, box 2 – bundle of letters from Rawdon-Brown.

33   ibid., Folder of Smirke letters, undated specification, probably 1863; General Accounts 5–6.

the ceiling, which survives, too insignificant for the room.[34] In November 1870 he began putting books on the library shelves and choosing soft furnishings.[35]

Creating the Landscape Setting

The landscape was seriously damaged by seven years (1813–19) of civil engineering, including much earth moving to provide the elevated platform for the new building. The great lake, planned in 1813, was slow to be realised. It would have disguised the raw slopes beneath the terraces but an estate plan of 1816 shows it as no more than a serpentine ribbon, not yet touching the lower flanks of the castle hill; even when the first prints appeared *c*. 1820, the lake was well below its modern level, the castle appearing to perch awkwardly on its unclothed mount. The 'pond head' or dam on the eastern perimeter was in need of constant attention until well into the 1820s, and a grand cascade rarely performed to the second earl's high expectations. Throughout the century the main impediment to developing the lake fully was the stable block attached to Castleditch, which remained in use long after the old house had been demolished in 1814.[36]

Between 1816 and 1826, nurserymen from Bristol, Gloucester and Hereford delivered parcels of herbaceous and shrubby plants, together with several hundred beech, elm, lime, horse chestnut, larch, and Weymouth pine trees, to border the gravel paths encircling the terraces. The number of gardeners rose from eight in 1818 to fifteen in 1821, including women and boys in busy seasons.[37] An empty envelope among Smirke's correspondence is endorsed with the name 'Repton', whose involvement, if any before his death in 1818, is likely to have been transitory.[38] In fact, the development of the landscape was probably subject to several influences. The head gardener, William Moss, was probably a man of some reflection, since he subscribed to William Dean's *Hortus Croomensis* (1828) which catalogued the recent planting at Lord Coventry's Worcestershire estate. George Watson, the land agent who was often left to make decisions while Lord Somers was abroad or staying in London or at Reigate Priory (Surrey), had a garden at Bronsil Cottage that was the epitome of the Regency style.[39] Two women in the Somers household may also have been influential: the Countess Somers, née Margaret Nash, whose father, the Revd Treadway Nash, developed an eclectic landscape garden around his Worcestershire villa, and her daughter, Lady Margaret, a published poet.[40] Lady Margaret exchanged poetry, much of it inspired

34   Eastnor Castle Mun., Letters to Virginia, 19 Nov. 1869.
35   ibid., 3 Nov. 1870, 21 Aug. 1871, 13 May 1873; Lady Henry Somerset (ed.), *Eastnor Castle* (1869), 32–4. They included tapestries viewed in Genoa in 1873, perhaps those later used in the library.
36   Eastnor Castle Mun., Smirke Accounts, passim; J.P. Neale, *Views of the seats of noblemen and gentlemen in England, Wales, Scotland and Ireland* 5 (1819), p. 2.
37   Eastnor Castle Mun., Estate Accounts, boxes 1–3.
38   ibid., Smirke letters (recently separated from the first Earl's correspondence). Between 1816 and 1818 at Armley House near Leeds. Smirke's new house was built in Repton's new landscape, see S. Daniels, *Humphry Repton* (1999), 245–50.
39   See picture above, Settlement, Domestic Buildings, Fig. 3.
40   Eastnor Castle Mun., Letters of Margaret Nash, Countess Somers, Box 1; Letters of Margaret and Mary Cox inc. letters from Elizabeth Barrett 1829–38.

by the local countryside, with her friend Elizabeth Barrett, herself a close friend of Uvedale Price of Foxley whose *Essays on the Picturesque* she read and admired.[41] The grounds at Miss Barrett's home, Hope End, Wellington Heath, had been laid out from 1809 in romantic style by J.C. Loudon, a disciple of Price.[42] Elizabeth Barrett also visited Mrs Watson at Bronsil Cottage, calling on the way at Eastnor, which she found rather intimidating.[43] So, although the first earl may have envisaged an austere and noble setting, creating an awe-inspiring effect of the kind initiated in the 1770s at Downton Castle by Richard Payne Knight,[44] by the 1840s taste for the sublime had succumbed to that for the picturesque. In the picture included in the estate survey of 1840, the castle seems to be enveloped with planting.

The wider landscape was also transformed. Charles Somers Cocks, who became the third Earl Somers in 1852, spent the 1840s travelling in the eastern Mediterranean with Layard.[45] Their trip to Algeria in 1843 sparked the earl's passion for introducing into

Figure 9 *The Castle and lake from the air c. 1930, seen from the north-east looking from the courtyard and main entrance to the lake beyond. The Great Hall rises in the middle of the roofscape.*

41   C. Watkins, *Uvedale Price: Decoding the Picturesque* (2012), 91–6.
42   D. Whitehead, *A Survey of the Historic Parks and Gardens of Herefordshire* (2001), 215–16.
43   P. Kelley & R. Hudson (eds), *Diary by E.B.B.* (1969), 46–7, 169–70.
44   Brooks and Pevsner, *Herefordshire* (2012), 206–7.
45   Eastnor Castle Mun., TS. notes by Dorothy Simmons quoting Layard correspondence and memoir, third Earl's correspondence, box 2.

the still, bare landscape to the south of the castle the exotic trees which remain one of the main attractions of the Eastnor estate.[46] In 1847 his sister, Lady Harriet, wrote 'your young trees (are) all flourishing (and) the garden is celebrated for possessing those Algerian shrubs [probably Atlas cedars] you brought over'. Lord Somers also cleared and planted the more distant parkland above Bronsil to carry the eye up to the bare slopes of the Malverns and to relate the castle for the first time to the Herefordshire countryside.[47]

By the 1860s, Smirke's terraces, which had been built in straitened circumstances, looked rather insignificant, as did the gravel walks laid out below them for convenience in the 1820s. Lower terraces were slowly constructed during that decade, but their finish was not decided upon until June 1875 when, at the third earl's suggestion, to test the effect Fox produced a series of large-scale canvasses, which were 'stretched up around the rock garden'.[48] The appearance of Renaissance-style defences was created by reticent crenellations above a corbel-table on the highest of the terraces. The final touches were not made until after 1883 when Fox was recalled by the third earl's daughter, Lady Henry Somerset, to design a wall fountain with four niches, a version of an original at Viterbo (Italy).[49] Lady Henry Somerset was also responsible for a new stable and garage block, built c. 1900 in the manner of C.F.A.Voysey.[50] The sixth Baron Somers continued his predecessor's interest in the gardens and park, making the park a setting for some of his social work in the 1930s.[51]

The family vacated the Castle during the Second World War, and when they returned in 1945 occupied only part of the building, which had been neglected as the family fortunes declined, a result of late 19th-century agricultural depression and 20th-century death duties. Some essential repairs were carried out by the Hon. Elizabeth Somers Cocks (d. 1986) and her husband Benjamin Hervey-Bathurst, but it was not until 1988 when James Hervey-Bathurst and his family moved into the Castle that restoration of house and grounds began in earnest.[52]

46   ibid., third Earl's correspondence with Harriet Prosser née Somers, box 2; W.J. Bean, *Trees and Shrubs* I (8th edn., 1970), p. 558.

47   Eastnor Castle Mun., General Accounts, vols 1–7 provide a comprehensive research tool for the Eastnor landscape in the 19th century and include a large collection of nurserymen's bills. A second collection (Grounds and Trees, boxes 1–2) is dedicated to the pleasure grounds and parkland; it also contains a collection of newspaper cuttings from the 19th-century gardening press relating to Eastnor.

48   Eastnor Castle Mun., Letters to Virginia, 20 June 1875.

49   Lady Somerset, *Eastnor Castle*, 45–6.

50   www.hiddenlives.org.uk/cgi-bin/displayrec.pl?searchtext=Eastnor&record=/homes/EASTN01.html, accessed 24 February 2012.

51   Hereford City Libr., Newspaper cuttings book no. 5, p. 7 (undated cutting); *The Times*, 12 May, 8 Aug. 1933 from digital archive infotrac.galegroup.com, accessed 4 July 2012; below, Social History.

52   www.eastnorcastle.com/history, accessed 16 July 2012.

ECONOMIC HISTORY

AGRICULTURE

EASTNOR HAS BEEN a predominantly agricultural parish throughout its history. Despite its hilly terrain, much of the parish, except for the area near the eastern boundary which was within the bishop's chase, was cultivated as arable land in the Middle Ages. In 1086 Domesday Book recorded a total of 18 ploughs or plough teams on the bishop's manor and its sub-manors, which covered the whole parish and some adjoining parts of Ledbury;[1] whether these were actual or notional ploughs or teams, the figure implies extensive arable. In the 1240s twelve oxen were required to cultivate the bishop's Eastnor manor, presumably his own directly-farmed land (demesne), the same number as on his larger Ledbury and Bosbury manors, although at Ledbury there was also a horse and at Bosbury another draught animal.[2] In 1404 there were two ploughlands (perhaps *c.* 240 a.) of arable on the bishop's Eastnor demesne.[3]

Arable Fields

In the western and central areas of the parish agricultural holdings were divided among several fields, blocks of strips (furlongs), and crofts of varying sizes which may have been cultivated in two or more separate systems, one in the north and another one or more in the south of the parish. For instance, land granted to St Katherine's hospital *c.* 1240 was held in selions (strips of arable) divided between seven fields or crofts, including Brankswell and Horsecroft, in the north of the parish.[4] Another charter shows that in the later 13th century a Ledbury man's four acres of land in Eastnor were held in three groups of selions, all of which lay along the brook which runs from Mitchell to Eastnor lake: in Brankswell field, in Nether Withycroft, and in Underdown.[5] In 1321 Henry son of Thomas Martin acquired a moiety (half) of a field lying between Kydelesmore and the highway, just east of the modern Way End Street, and five selions in the Nether field, probably in the same area.[6] A small estate conveyed in 1349 comprised land, mainly

1   *Domesday Book, Herefordshire* (Phillimore, 1983), 2, 27 (f. 182).
2   *English Episcopal Acta* xxxv. *Hereford 1234–75*, ed. J. Barrow (British Academy, 2009), no. 87, p. 82.
3   *Cal. Inq. Misc.* vii (1339–1422), no. 281, p. 152.
4   DCA 3659.
5   ibid. 7018/3, p. 3.
6   HRO, CF50/178, Heref H 59 (Cal of BL Add Ch 72716).

in two-acre parcels, in seven fields or closes, all apparently in the south of the parish.[7] Seventeen acres held from Thomas Clinton in the mid 16th century comprised 3 a. in Great Withycroft, 2 a. in nearby Underdown, 5 a. in Branks field, and a total of 7 a. in Mitchell field.[8] In 1444, however, 3 a. were divided between Branks field, an unidentified Loveryngesacre, and 'Pyryeacre' which seems to have been at or near Goldhill, south of the site of Eastnor Castle.[9]

Sixteenth-century descriptions or surveys of the rector's land (glebe) and the Castleditch and bishop's demesnes suggest three divisions of the fields. The glebe in the 1570s was divided between three areas: land in or near Ridgeway field, straddling the boundary between Eastnor and Ledbury, with other land further west along the

Figure 10 *Former strips in Lower Bare Acre field, west of Clencher's Mill Lane, in 1726, with the names of their owners.*

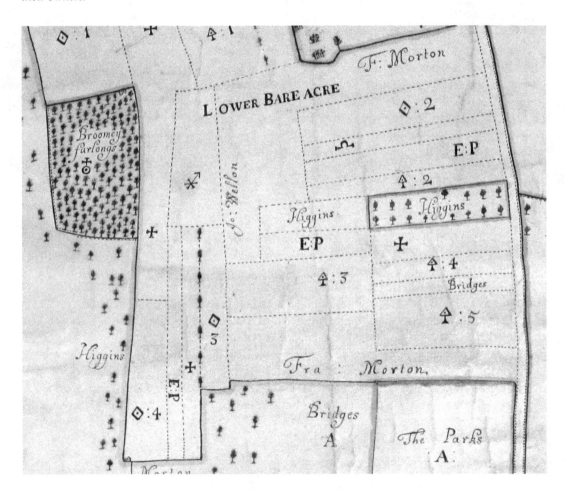

7   HRO, Heref H 91 (Cal of BL Add Ch 72747).
8   Eastnor Castle Mun., Castleditch box.
9   BL Add Ch 72844: reference supplied by John Freeman from EPNS notes; Eastnor Castle Mun., case 4, bundle 8: Old deeds Gold Hill estate.

boundary; land in or near Branks field west of the Ledbury road; and land in Bare Acre and Goldhill in the south of the parish. Much of the glebe was held in acre, two-acre and half-acre strips, but ten 'parcels' seem to have been inclosed.[10] The 114 a. of arable of the Castleditch demesne in 1606 were clearly divided between three fields or groups of fields: the Rye fields (38 a. 3r.) which lay mainly round the Ridgeway, Poulfield (34 a.) which seems to have lain around the manor house, and Fallow field (41 a. 2 r.) which seems to have been in the same area.[11] In 1578 the bishop's demesne arable was divided, rather unevenly, between the same three fields or groups of fields: 36 a. lay inclosed in Bare Acre south of the manor house, a total of 43 a. lay in or near Branks field, and a total of c. 58 a. in or near Ridgeway field.[12] The episcopal demesne was intermixed with the tenants' lands: land leased by Ivo Clinton to a husbandman in 1597 included two parcels of land in Ridgeway field, 'lying severally between the demesne lands of the bishop of Hereford on every side'.[13]

Grants of assarts, or land cleared for arable, at Deerfold (later part of Bronsil) show that by the mid to late 12th century some of the woodland near the eastern edge of the parish had been cleared, and at least part of it had been divided into yardlands, the traditional division of land in the common fields.[14] Other land in the same area seems to have been held as inclosed fields: in the mid 13th century two 'fields' called Broad field and Hod hill were held in their entirety with their hedges.[15] In 1343 William Blundel quitclaimed to his son a moiety of his estate in Eastnor, including land in Styweys field, Old field, Middle field, and Eden furlong, as well as two crofts; other named places included Deerfold which was certainly later part of the Bronsil estate.[16]

The manner in which these fields and crofts were organised for cultivation is not clear, but the three-course rotation common in eastern Herefordshire seems to have been followed in the later 13th century. The works due to the bishop from the customary tenants c. 1288 suggest a rotation of winter wheat, followed by oats and then fallow.[17] A labourer who died in 1664 had 4 a. of corn and 4 a. of lent grain at his death, suggesting that a three-course rotation was still being practised.[18]

Meadow

Only 6 a. of meadow was recorded in the bishop's demesne in 1086 and in the 1280s,[19] but charters record extensive meadow along the Glynch brook and its tributaries. The amount of meadow is confirmed by maps of the Clinton estate in 1726 which show

10 HRO, HD2/1/36, printed in Somers-Cocks, *Eastnor and Its Malvern Hills*, 196–207.
11 Eastnor Castle Mun., Castleditch box.
12 HRO, AA59 A2, ff. 98v., 99.
13 Eastnor Castle Mun., case 2, bundle 1B.
14 HRO, AH82/2–3.
15 ibid., AH82/6. For their location, HRO, CF50/178, Heref C87 (Cal of BL Add Ch 72740); DCA 7018/3, pp. 10–11.
16 HRO, CF50/178, Heref C76 (Cal of BL Add Ch 72736).
17 ibid., AA59 A1, p. 147.
18 Eastnor Castle Mun., case 2, bundle 7 (probate inventory).
19 *Domesday Book: Herefordshire* (Phillimore), 2, 27 (fol. 182); HRO, AA59 A1, p. 147.

meadows and leasows (grassland) along all the streams. Its name implies that Broad meadow on the Glynch brook, first recorded in the 13th century, was a large one, perhaps the same as the 9-acre Broad meadow described in the same area in 1692.[20] Meadow lower down the stream, at Clenchford, was sold in 1340.[21] Other charters show that more meadows lay along the Withy or Withycroft brook south of Mitchell, in Horsecroft and Gatleys meadow, and yet others extended further north along its tributary stream, Brankswell.[22] In the east of the parish there were meadows on the stream south of the Tewkesbury road, and at Bronsil.[23] Castleditch manor had c. 52 a. of meadow in demesne in 1606, and in 1770 the bishop of Hereford's Eastnor estate included 23 a. of meadow worth 15s. an acre.[24] In 1804 part of the St Katherine's estate contained c. 12 a. of meadow out of a total area of c. 32 a.[25]

In the royal charter granting the newly-created Bronsil estate to Richard Beauchamp in 1460, the estate was said to contain 200 a. of meadow, an improbably large area; a charter of 1469 described a more realistic 73 acres.[26] A map of the estate in 1726 shows only a little over 23 a. of meadow.[27] In 1772 a surveyor reported that five acres of meadow on the estate needed to be drained.[28]

In 1365 land in Gatleys meadow granted to St Katherine's hospital, Ledbury, was held 'indivisibly and in common', apparently in parcels or strips marked by boundary markers.[29] An acre of land in Setterne meadow along the Glynch brook in the 1570s was marked on one side by a mere stone and stakes. That and another meadow were half freehold and half customary (copyhold) land, the two halves being divided by cocks of hay at mowing time. A mid 15th-century lease of the same land stated that the tenant of the customary meadow was to mow both meadows and then have no more to do with the land until midsummer a year later.[30] Their names suggest that a close of meadow called Short Dole in 1625 and pasture called Camms Dole in 1630 were once lot meadow.[31]

Pasture

Charters show that some pasture, like the meadow, lay along the streams,[32] and was held in small parcels. Other pasture was on the higher ground particularly in the eastern half

20   DCA 1661; ibid. 7018, p. 22; Eastnor Castle Mun., case 4, bundle 8: Old deeds Gold Hill estate.
21   HRO, CF50/178, Heref DD 19 (Cal of BL Add Ch 72733).
22   DCA 3659, 3674; ibid. 7018/3, pp. 28–9.
23   HRO, AH82/5; ibid., CF50/178, Heref L 19 (Cal of Add Ch 72852).
24   Eastnor Castle Mun., Castleditch box; Eastnor Parish box 2.
25   DCA 3600.
26   *Cal. Chart R.* vi. (1427–1516), 137; *Cal. Close* Edw IV, vol. 2, no. 459; www.british-history.ac.uk, accessed 19 November 2009.
27   Eastnor Castle Mun., map of Bronsil 1726.
28   ibid., Bronsil box.
29   DCA 7018/3, pp. 28–9.
30   HRO, AA59 A2, f. 100v.
31   Eastnor Castle Mun., case 1, bundle 2, no. 1; Castleditch box.
32   e.g. DCA 585, 3664; HRO, AA59 A2, f. 99v.

of the parish. Eighteenth- and early 19th-century maps suggest that much of it was wood pasture.[33] The rental of *c.* 1288 records *c.* 17 a. of pasture in demesne on the bishop's manor, but an enquiry into the bishop's lands found only 2 a. in 1404.[34] The amount of pasture probably increased in the late Middle Ages. The Bronsil estate was mainly grass or wood in 1460; its name implies that one pasture, called le Stocking in 1459,[35] had been cleared from woodland. A parcel of pasture recorded in the survey of the bishop's lands in 1578 seems to have been in or near the modern Eastnor park.[36] In 1650 the Gullet, on the Malvern hills on the eastern parish boundary, contained 73 a. of pasture.[37] Pasture at Howler's Heath was first certainly recorded in 1619,[38] but the high ground there, like the Malvern Hills, was probably always used for grazing.

There was a stint (ration of animals) for grazing, at least in parts of the parish, for in 1556 William Mitchell was accused of overburdening the common, and *c.* 1580 the rector had common for 20 sheep in the common fields, and common 'according to his arable lands' elsewhere.[39] A conveyance in 1710 of meadow in Hill field, just north of Howler's Heath, included common of pasture for all cattle 'in Hill Field and in Eastnor.'[40] In 1770 Hill End and Joiner's farms in the south-east of the parish had right of common on Howler's Heath, and Dolitch farm in the north had rights on 'Malvern Hill'.[41]

Woodland

In 1086 the bishop's manor contained woodland 4 furlongs by 2 furlongs; some of the wood or charcoal produced may have been sent to Droitwich, where the manor had part of a salt pan, to provide fuel for salt-making.[42] In 1323 there was wood at 'Kydeleyesmor',[43] probably near the Tewkesbury road east of Way End. Wood at Howler's Heath was recorded in 1330, Birch wood, just west of the later Bronsil Castle, in 1345, and Over wood, apparently in the south of the parish, in 1364.[44] The land to be emparked at Bronsil in 1460 included an improbable 600 a. of wood, including Dryfawd or Deerfold, which had been described as a wood in 1459, and 11 a. of wood at Netherhook and Overhook.[45] A detailed description of the estate in 1469 recorded a total of 141 a. of

33   Eastnor Castle Mun., maps of Bronsil 1726, 1808, and (for Howler's Heath) of 'Estates in the parish of Eastnor', 1808.

34   HRO, AA59 A1, p. 147; *Cal. Inq. Misc.* vii (1339–1422), no. 281, p. 152.

35   HRO, CF50/178, Heref F 28 (Cal of BL Add Ch 72851); *Cal. Chart R.* vi. (1427–1516), 137.

36   HRO, AA59 A2, f. 102v.

37   M.G. Watkins, *Collections for the History and Antiquities of Herefordshire, Radlow Hundred* (1902) bound as Duncomb's *Herefordshire* vol. 5, p. 84.

38   Eastnor Castle Mun., case 2, bundle 2.

39   HRO, AM33/4; ibid., HD2/1/36, printed in Somers-Cocks, *Eastnor and its Malvern Hills*, 196–207.

40   Eastnor Castle Mun., case 2, bundle B.

41   ibid., Eastnor Estates box 11, Nathaniel Kent survey.

42   *Domesday Book: Herefordshire*, 2,27 (f. 182a); H.C. Darby, *Domesday England* (Cambridge 1986), 261.

43   HRO, AH82/8.

44   ibid., CF50/178, Heref C 12 (Cal of BL Add Ch 72726), Heref C 8 (Cal of BL Add Ch 72740), Heref DD 31 (Cal of BL Add Ch 72769).

45   *Cal. Chart R.* vi. (1427–1516), 137; HRO, CF50/178, Heref L 19 (Cal of Add Ch 72852), Heref L 23, 24 (Cal of BL Add Ch 72871–2).

woodland.[46] In 1500 a grant of a house and enclosed land at Howlers allowed the tenant to burn charcoal, provided that half the profit went to Lord Beauchamp.[47]

The Eastnor woodlands, like others in the county, were carefully managed.[48] In the mid 17th century News Wood and the Ridings on the Hospital estate, totalling c. 20 a., were coppice, felled after 15 years; at least part of the timber was made into charcoal.[49] In 1726 the Castleditch estate contained a total of 157 a. of woodland in Eastnor, and a small area of coppice in the north-east corner of the Mitchell estate in Ledbury.[50] The Bronsil estate in that year included part of Birching Wood and one three-acre coppice; by 1808 Rough Leasowe (20 a.) in the north of the estate had been converted to coppice.[51] When Nathaniel Kent surveyed the Castleditch estate in 1770, there were c. 118 a. of coppiced woodland in Eastnor, cut on 13- and 14-year cycles. Kent recommended clearing and breaking up 80 a. of Birching Wood for arable,[52] work which was being carried out in 1772 when c. 40 a. of the former wood was to be broken up and sown with corn for a few years.[53] A survey of the Eastnor estate in 1808 listed 23 coppices in Eastnor and a further 23 in Ledbury. All the Ledbury coppices and most of the Eastnor ones were felled on a 13-year cycle.[54] In 1838 there was 369 a. of coppice woodland in the parish.[55]

Inclosure

Some piecemeal inclosure of parcels of land in the common fields took place in the late Middle Ages and the 16th century; by the time of Butterfield's survey of the bishop's manor in 1578 an area of 36 a. of demesne arable in Bare Acre had been inclosed.[56] In 1670 three acres, apparently arable, had lately been inclosed out of Willow Croft (Withycroft) field, and in 1681 three ridges (½ a.) of arable land had recently been inclosed out of Westbrook field. Two three-acre inclosures of arable land taken from common fields in the part of Ledbury parish north of Eastnor were conveyed in 1712.[57] In 1738 arable land in Bare Acre field had been inclosed and planted with fruit trees.[58] However, a conveyance of 1768 shows that Underdown was then still a 'common field', and arable in it was held in parcels of 2 a., 1 a., and ½ a.; in the early 19th century the lands of one small estate, probably in the north of the parish, were 'scattered among Lord Somers's lands'.[59] A survey of the St Katherine's hospital estate in 1804 noted that

46   *Cal. Close.* 1468–76, 459.
47   HRO, CF50/178, Heref J 36 (Cal. of unidentified Shrewsbury/Talbot deed).
48   e.g. B. Lewis, 'A History of Mowley Wood at Staunton-on-Arrow', *TWNFC* (2002), 347–55.
49   TNA, E 134/1657/MICH3.
50   Eastnor Castle Mun., maps of Castleditch and Mitchell, 1726.
51   ibid., maps of Bronsil 1726, 1808.
52   ibid., Eastnor Estates box 11, Nathaniel Kent survey.
53   ibid., Bronsil box.
54   ibid., Eastnor Estates box 10.
55   TNA, IR 18/3030.
56   HRO, AA59 A2, f. 98.
57   Eastnor Castle Mun., case 3, unnumbered box, bundle 51 (Whitehouse), no. 11; ibid., case 2, bundle 1B.
58   ibid., case 2, bundle 1A.
59   ibid., case 3, unlabelled box.

several small parcels of arable land should be exchanged or 'laid together', and as late as 1812 the hospital estate of *c.* 119 acres was 'much scattered and intermixed with Lord Somers's property'.[60]

Similar piecemeal inclosure took place in the meadow and pasture. In 1621 half an acre of meadow and two small parcels of pasture on the St Katherine's hospital estate in Netherton had both been inclosed.[61] Meadow in Withycroft had been inclosed before 1670.[62] In 1788 three quarters of an acre of meadow had 'lately' been inclosed out of Underdown field.[63] Seven acres of pasture on Midsummer Hill had recently been inclosed in 1775.[64]

Almost the whole parish had been inclosed by 1813 when, presumably at the instigation of Lord Somers, an Act was obtained for the inclosure of *c.* 180 a. of commons or waste, and of 'certain open and common fields of the parish'. The 185 a. of land inclosed under the resultant award was almost all common pasture on Midsummer Hill, Howler's Heath and other high ground in Eastnor, although the Act also covered a small area of Ledbury parish north of Eastnor and also Dingwood Park in the extreme south of Ledbury parish, all areas in which Earl Somers was the chief landowner. Most of the award was concerned with a series of exchanges to create consolidated blocks of land for the different owners, principally for the earl.[65] In having such a small proportion of its land subject to parliamentary inclosure, Eastnor was not untypical of Herefordshire parishes, many of which had Acts for even smaller areas; at nearby Bosbury, with an area 4816 a., *c.* 105 a. of arable and meadow were inclosed in 1854 and 7 a. of common in 1865.[66]

Crops and Livestock

The works to be performed by some of the bishop's tenants, listed in the rental of *c.* 1288, imply that wheat and oats were sown in spring,[67] but otherwise there is no evidence for medieval crops. One of the Castleditch demesne fields was called the Rye field in 1606, presumably from its crop, and a pasture close called Barley close in 1692 may once have been sown with that grain.[68]

Wills of the 16th and 17th centuries confirm the practice of mixed farming suggested by the amount of recorded arable and pasture. A husbandman in 1591 had wheat, rye, beans, apples, and honey, as well as two cows, a calf, 16 sheep, pigs, and poultry; a yeoman in 1617 left peas and barley in addition to four ewes and lambs.[69] Another man in 1667 bequeathed barley, oats, and beans as well as 53 sheep. Several testators

60   DCA 3600.
61   Eastnor Castle Mun., case 4, terrier of Netherton.
62   ibid., case 3, unnumbered box, bundle 51 (Whitehouse), no. 10.
63   ibid., case 1, bundle 8.
64   ibid., case 1, bundle 5.
65   ibid., Eastnor Parish box 2 (includes copy of Act); HRO, Q/R1/17.
66   P. Farquhar-Oliver, unpublished paper on 'Parliamentary Enclosures in Herefordshire' (2003–4); W.E. Tate, 'A Hand List of English Enclosure Awards, Part 15: Herefordshire', *TWNFC* (1939), 183–94.
67   HRO, AA59 A1, pp. 146–7.
68   Eastnor Castle Mun., Castleditch box ; ibid., case 4, bundle 8: Old deeds Gold Hill estate.
69   HRO, 6/5/64, will of Richard Bache 1591; ibid., 33/3/9 will of Thomas Baulden 1617.

had muncorn (mixed grain), and one in 1687 rye.[70] A carpenter who died in 1694 had a dozen acres of corn and 40 a. of pulse; his livestock comprised 8 bullocks and oxen, 14 cattle, 6 two-year old heifers, 4 yearlings, 6 calves, 140 sheep, and 20 pigs.[71] One woman bequeathed a stall of bees in 1565.[72] The gentleman Humphrey Morton who died in 1671 had 9 plough oxen to cultivate his arable, 17 cows and a bull and 17 other cattle; he kept 78 sheep on one farm and a further 68 in a sheep cot.[73] A cow called Fillpail in 1579 was clearly a good milker.[74]

Fruit-growing is recorded from the 13th century when the new owner of a croft was forbidden to cut down pear trees in the boundary hedges.[75] In 1544 the tenant of Bronsil Castle was forbidden to grub up apple, pear or crab trees.[76] By 1715 a total of 5½ a. of land in Bare Acre field, north-west of Clenchford mill, had been planted with fruit trees, and maps of 1726 show orchards at Massington, Woodwards End, Rowick, and Cowley's End farms, as well as extensive plantations of fruit trees to the west and south of Castleditch.[77] Three acres of land on the edge of the Malvern hills had recently been planted with fruit trees in 1771.[78]

Hops were being grown in the parish by 1637 when the Thomas Higgins of Hillend, gentleman, left to his wife (among other lands) hopyards at Woolpits on the boundary between Ledbury and Eastnor.[79] Land in Eastnor was called Whiller's Hopyard in 1671, and a deed of 1675 suggests that an acre of grass had recently been made into a hopyard, but in 1726 a hopyard had apparently been converted to grass.[80] A hop room was to be built at Upper Mitchell farm, on the Ledbury part of the Eastnor estate, c. 1805, and in 1828 growing hops were damaged by a wet spring.[81] In 1841 there were 9 a. of hops on the estate; hop-pickers were employed at Upper Mitchell farm in 1893.[82]

In 1792 the arable on the Lowes Hurst estate in the north of the parish was sown with c. 9 a. of wheat, c. 5 a. of peas, c. 3 a. of beans, and c. 2 a. of barley, probably as part of a three-course rotation. A nine-year lease of Hill farm, granted in 1764, required the tenant to muck and dung the fields, to spread lime on the arable, and to keep young trees safe from cattle and sheep; in the last spring of the lease he was to sow 4 a. of land with 32 lb. of clover seed.[83] Leases of several farms on the Eastnor estate in 1808 forbade the planting of hemp, flax or rape, or other impoverishing seeds without the landlord's permission, and the ploughing up of meadow or hop ground without licence. Tenants were required

70   HRO, 15/2/46, will of Thomas Pewtress 1667; ibid. 16/2/60, will of John Elcox 1588; ibid. 44/1/55, will of
     John Webley 1592; ibid., 99/4/15 will of Thomas Richards 1687.
71   ibid., 118/3/35, inventory of William Burroppe 1694.
72   ibid., 23/1/33, will of Jane Hopley, 1565.
73   ibid., 29/1/44, inventory of Humphrey Morton 1671.
74   ibid., 6/4/19 will of Alice Bache, 1579.
75   ibid., AH82/4.
76   Eastnor Castle Mun., Bronsil box.
77   ibid., case 2, bundle 1A; ibid. maps of Castleditch and Mitchell, 1726.
78   ibid., case 2, bundle 7.
79   HRO, 49/3/5, will of Thomas Higgins, 1637.
80   Eastnor Castle Mun, case 1, bundle 2, no. 12; bundle 5; case 2, bundle B.
81   ibid., Eastnor Estates box 10.
82   TNA, IR 18/3030; HRO, M5B/15/2.
83   Eastnor Castle Mun., case 1, bundles 4, 7.

to preserve fruit trees from cattle and to plant new apple, pear and crab stocks in place of any injured trees. At the last Michaelmas of the lease the tenant was not to sow more than a third of the arable with wheat, and that only after a summer fallow or a planting with clover. At the final spring planting he was to sow part of the arable with clover and other grass seed. At the end of the lease tenants were to leave hop grounds well worked, their ditches scoured, and 'sufficient quantity of good poles stripped, sharped and piled' to 'poll' the hop grounds.[84]

In 1801 just over half the arable under crop in the parish, 252 a. out of 266 a., was reported to have been sown with wheat, 74 a. with oats, 41 a. with beans, 34 a. with peas, 33 a. with barley, 23 a. with turnips, 6 a. with potatoes, and 3 a. with rye.[85] In 1838 a 5-course rotation of (1) wheat (2) beans (3) oats or barley (4) clover or vetches and (5) fallow was followed. The livestock kept on the extensive pasture comprised 60 cows, 150 bullocks, 40 horses, and 2,000 sheep.[86]

Farms

The leading surveyor Nathaniel Kent reported on Sir Charles Cocks's estates in 1770.[87] His survey covered c. 1258 a. in Eastnor, divided into the demesne lands and 12 farms, and a further 543 a. in Ledbury on Mitchell, Massington, Ockeridge and Netherton farms. Only a third of Sir Charles's agricultural land in Eastnor and about a quarter of that in Ledbury was arable, the rest being meadow or pasture, including 90 a. in the Park at Eastnor. Most of the farms similarly had more grass than arable land. The exceptions were farms in the north and south of Eastnor parish. The Hill farm, which extended into Bromsberrow (Glos.), had 44½ a. of arable to 31½ a. of grass; the nearby Howlers farm and the very small Beaches, both held by the same tenant, had 46 a. to 36½ a. and 9 a. to 4 a. of arable to pasture respectively; Dolitch, later part of Fowlet farm, had 14 a. of arable to 12 a. of pasture. White House farm in the north of the parish had 48½ a. of arable to 42½ a. of grass. Much of the pasture was in poor condition and required draining; land on Hill farm needed liming. Beaches, Howlers, and Hillend farms produced large quantities of cider.

In the 19th century the cultivated land in Eastnor parish was divided between 8–10 farms. The home farm of the Eastnor estate covered a total area of c. 204 a., including 94 a. of arable, when the bishop exchanged it with Lord Somers in 1770.[88] The chief tenanted farms were at Goldhill, White House, Fowlet, Martins, Hill, Hillend, Beacon and Upper House. In addition the Somers Cocks family owned Woolpits, Upper and Lower Mitchell, Massington, Netherton and Ockeridge in adjoining parts of Ledbury. In 1808 the highest rent on the Castleditch estate was paid by Thomas Higgins for a group of farms including Rowicks, Joiners, Howlers, Hillend and Clencher's mill.[89] Hillend farm,

84 Eastnor Castle Mun., case 1, bundle 12.
85 *Home Office Acreage Returns* (HO67) (List & Index Soc. 189, 1982), 220.
86 TNA, IR 18/3030.
87 Eastnor Castle Mun., Eastnor Estates box 11, survey by Nathaniel Kent.
88 ibid., Eastnor Parish box 2.
89 ibid., Eastnor Estates box 10.

Figure 11 *Threshing beans with a flail at Eastnor in 1898.*

274 a., was the largest in the parish in 1851, but was not recorded after 1861, when it had
been reduced to 80 acres. Goldhill, at 85 a. one of the smaller farms in 1851, within 20
years had grown to be the largest farm in the parish, with 750 a. in 1871 and 648 a. in 1881.
Hill farm (120 a. in 1861 and 200 a. in 1871) and Fowlet farm (130 a. in 1851 and 140 a. in
1861) were the only other farms usually over 100 a. in extent.[90] In 1890 one farmer rented
c. 462 a. from the Eastnor estate, including Goldhill, Martins, and Ockeridge farms, an
unsatisfactory arrangement.[91]

From about the mid 19th century the Eastnor estate embarked on a modernisation of
many of its farm buildings, investing in new barns, stables, cattle sheds, pigsties, cart sheds,
wagon sheds and cider houses. The buildings confirm the practice of mixed farming, with
barns and granaries used for crops, cow houses and yards for cattle. Most are of stone
with brick dressings to openings, and the most extensive are at Eastnor Farm, the home
farm of the estate. The covered cattle yards at Eastnor Farm and at the Somers Arms and
the cow houses at Goldhill Farm, Hill Farm, Upper House Farm, and at Upper Mitchell
and Netherton Farms in Ledbury demonstrate the importance of cattle on the estate. The
Upper House Farm cow house would have held six animals, that at Netherton nine, and

90   TNA, HO 107/1975; ibid. RG 9/1808; RG 10/2682; RG 11/2581.
91   Eastnor Castle Mun., Eastnor box 15.

that at Upper Mitchell eleven, possibly including three calves. Additional hop kilns were built at Upper Mitchell Farm in about the 1870s and at White House Farm c.1886.[92]

In the early 1940s there were 11 farms: Home farm, Clencher's Mill, Hill (in the south of the parish), Fowlet, Beacon, Goldhill, Upper House, White House, Somers Arms, Hill House (in the north of the parish) and Netherton (partly in Ledbury).[93] The chief development since 1900 was the great increase in the size of Home farm which had grown to 720 a. The next largest farms were Goldhill (403 a.), Netherton (268 a.), Hill House (256 a.) and White House (254 a.); two other farms were c. 120 a. each, and the remaining five were between 40 a. and 100 a. There were also six smallholdings, each under 15 a. The farmer at Hill House also held Upper Mitchell (c. 250 a.) in Ledbury, and he or another man of the same name farmed at White House; the farmer at Goldhill also occupied land belonging to the estate in Gloucestershire.

The cropping was very similar to that of previous centuries. Despite 111 a. of old pasture having been ploughed up in 1941 on government instructions, the total area

Figure 12 *Cider mill in a late 18th- or early 19th-century building at White House Farm in 2010.*

---

92 J.E.C. Peters, unpublished report on Eastnor farm buildings; idem, 'The Origins of the Covered Yard, *Historic Farm Buildings Group Review* (Winter 2007), 13–17.
93 TNA, MAF 32/8/153. The remaining paragraphs of this section were drafted by Dr Sylvia Pinches.

under crops in 1942, 405 a., was less than the 466 a. in 1801 and 490 a. in 1838.[94] Only Clencher's Mill had more than a third of land under crop, the majority of farms had less than a fifth. Grain crops were the most important, with 134½ a. of wheat, 54½ a. of oats, 34½ a. of barley and 44½ a. of mixed grain. There were 60½ a. of fodder crops, 18 a. of potatoes, 10 a. of hops (at White House), 6 a. of sugar beet and 1 a. of rape. Orchards occupied 58 a., soft fruit 3 a., and vegetables for market just over 1 a. The permanent grass comprised 1284 a. of pasture and 338 a. of grass for mowing.

Stocking, too, followed previous patterns, with a preponderance of sheep (1693 on 12 of the holdings) over cattle (513 on 13 of the holdings). Ten farms had milking cows, but only five of them had ten or more; other stock was being raised for slaughter. Five farms had large flocks of poultry. Ten farms used horses, although five of them also had tractors.

In the course of the later 20th century there was considerable amalgamation and reorganisation of the farms. In 2010 only the southern Hill farm, Upper House with Fowlet and Netherton were occupied and worked by tenant farmers. The northern Hill (House) Farm was farmed with Lower Mitchell and Bradlow farms in Ledbury. Goldhill, Beacon, Clencher's Mill, Bronsil, Somers Arms, and White House were all farmed directly by the estate. At Bronsil, Beacon, and Somers Arms farms the buildings were let separately to commercial enterprises, as were most of the Home farm buildings.

Mills and Ponds

There were at least three watermills in Eastnor in the later Middle Ages and the 16th century: Castleditch mill and Clenchford (later Clencher's) mill on the Glynch, and Bronsil mill on the stream near Bronsil castle. The bishop's watermill, Clencher's mill, was let for 4 marks (£2 3s. 4d.) c. 1288, but in 1404 it was valued at only 6s. 8d. a year.[95] In 1497 and 1524 it was being leased, with its adjoining land, to Lord Richard Beauchamp for 20s. a year.[96] In 1578 the mill was a water and a fulling mill; in 1764, a double water corn mill.[97] The miller went out of business in 1889, perhaps because the buildings were old and the water supply at times inadequate.[98] A new water supply, established in 1907, powered the mill until the 1920s, by which time it was used only to make animal feed. The mill, then powered by a tractor, finally ceased working c. 1960.[99] The surviving early 19th-century brick and weather-boarded building encases an earlier timber-framed structure. Some of the machinery, still in working order, is 18th-century, and the iron waterwheel bears the date 1820. The stone-built two-storeyed mill house is of the early 19th century.[100]

The mill on Bronsil manor was first recorded in 1495, and 'Bromhill mill' and its meadow were included in a lease of the castle and estate in 1544, but excluded from a

---

94   *Home Office Acreage Returns* (HO67) (List and Index Society, vol. 189, 1982), 220; TNA, IR 18/3030.
95   HRO, AA59 A1, p. 145; *Cal. Inq. Misc.* vii (1339–1422), no. 281, p. 152; for the name, *Reg. Trefnant*, 165.
96   HRO, AM33/12; AM33/15.
97   ibid., AA59 A2, f. 101; Eastnor Castle Mun., case 2, bundle 6.
98   *London Gazette* 3 Jan. 1890, p. 44; Eastnor Castle Mun., Eastnor Estates box 15.
99   HRO, M5B/15/4; information sheet from Eastnor Estate.
100 National Heritage List 1082624; information from Mr Alan Stoyel.

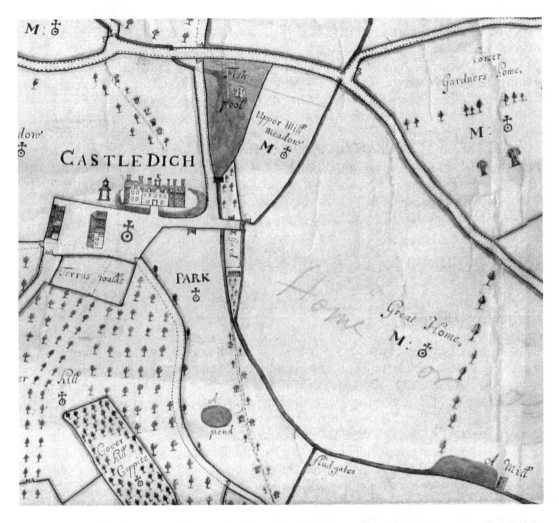

Figure 13 *Castleditch House and its surroundings, showing a dovecote and outbuildings as well as its fish pool, mill and meadows, 1726.*

sale in 1555.[101] There is no later record of the mill, although Bronsil estate maps of 1726 and 1808 show a Mill Meadow just north of the Tewkesbury road.[102] The 'lower' mill, held on lease from the bishop by Sir Gilbert Talbot of Bronsil in 1537,[103] was presumably a different mill, probably the lower mill on the Glynch shown on the Castleditch estate map of 1726.

In 1606 the Castleditch estate included two mills which, like Clencher's Mill, lay on the Glynch. The 1726 estate map shows Upper Mill meadow, a large fishpond, and a building which could well have been a mill near Castleditch house, and a mill and Lower

101 BL Add Ch 72891 (reference supplied by John Freeman from EPNS notes); Eastnor Castle Mun., Bronsil box.
102 Eastnor Castle Mun., maps of Bronsil 1726, 1808.
103 TNA, SC 6/HenVIII/1511, rot. 11d..

Mill meadow on the north-east bank of the river near Goldhill.[104] There is no later record of either mill.

Charters record land in Eastnor which lay 'towards' the windmill in 1388 and a windmill, probably near the Ledbury boundary, in 1467. It may have been the predecessor of the windmill in Upper Windmill field in Mitchell, shown on a map of 1726.[105]

The rental of *c.* 1288 records that four of the bishop's tenants paid an annual rent 'for fish', and 'fish silver' was due to the bishop in 1524. The payments were presumably for use of fishponds, like those paid by tenants on Castleditch manor for fishing at two pools and in 'certain pits' in 1630.[106] The pond at Castleditch house shown on the map of 1726 was a fishpond.[107] Pools in Bronsil park had been let separately from the castle and its land in 1555, and a rectangular pond in a field north of the castle was shown on the 1726 map.[108]

INDUSTRY AND CRAFTS

Early Occupations

Until the later 19th century the few people in the parish not engaged in agriculture worked mostly in service trades, like the members of the Gateley family who, charters show, were bakers in 1327 and tailors in 1382 and 1390.[109] A carpenter recorded in 1414, and a wheelwright in 1687, probably worked on farms, like the cooper who lived in the parish in 1712 and 1715, and the two thatchers, both members of the same family, recorded in 1801.[110] The five shoemakers recorded between 1565 and 1729[111] would have served the local population, but the cordwainer who moved into the parish from Ledbury in 1752 and the others recorded between then and 1824 made better quality shoes,[112] presumably for a wider market. The four glovers recorded between 1661 and 1694 may have worked for Ledbury masters, as presumably did the four weavers and two narrow weavers recorded between 1582 and 1755.[113]

---

104 Eastnor Castle Mun., Castleditch box; ibid., case 2, bundle B; ibid., Castleditch map 1726.

105 HRO, CF50/178, Heref II 17 (Cal of Talbot/Shrewsbury deed); BL Add MS 46458, f.6; Eastnor Castle Mun., Mitchell map 1726.

106 HRO, AA59 A1, p. 146; ibid., AM33/15; Eastnor Castle Mun., Castleditch box.

107 Eastnor Castle Mun., Castleditch map 1726.

108 ibid., Bronsil box; Bronsil map 1726.

109 HRO, CF50/178, Heref H 7 (Cal of Talbot/Shrewsbury deed); Heref DD 41 (BL Add Ch 72789); Heref DD 42 (Cal of BL Add Ch 72797).

110 ibid., CF50/178, Heref FF 29 (Cal of BL Add Ch 72818); Eastnor Castle Mun., case 1, bundle 9; case 2, bundles 1A, 1B, B.

111 HRO, 12/2/20, will of William Clifton, 1565; Eastnor Castle Mun., case 2, bundles 1A, 1B, 2, 7; case 3, box 1, bundle 42.

112 Eastnor Castle Mun., case 1, bundle 9; case 2, bundles 4, 7; case 3, box 1, bundle 60.

113 ibid., case 1, bundle 2, no. 18; case 2, bundles 1A, 1B; case 3, box 1, bundles 25, 37; case 4, unnumbered box, bundle 56; HRO, 17/4/12, will of William Batch, 1612; 43/4/14, will of Leonard Branche, 1632.

The Llandovery sandstone used in the ramparts of Midsummer Hill fort was quarried at Bronsil.[114] In the late 16th century there was usable stone on the Netherton estate, and 'quarry' field names were recorded in Eastnor in 1606 and 1746.[115] Robert Sandford occupied a stone quarry on the Hill farm in 1764 and a limestone quarry near Clencher's mill, possibly the same one, in 1772.[116] There were quarries on the St Katherine's hospital estate in 1805, and on Lord Somers's land at Lower Mitchell in 1808.[117] In 1835 a quarry or quarries in the park produced 'good limestone . . . from which beautiful marble is obtained'.[118] Hollybush quarry on the edge of the Malverns, recorded in 1913, remained in operation until the early 1970s; the nearby Gullet closed in 1974.[119] In 1582 the tenant of a tin mine in Eastnor or Colwall hoped it might produce gold. There is no further record of a mine at Eastnor, although attempts to find gold near the Wyche in Colwall continued into the early 18th century.[120]

A charter granted land in a lime pit field in the parish in 1364.[121] In 1581 a lime kiln at Netherton was let at 'no trifling rent', and others were recorded in 1738 and 1805.[122] In the early 19th century there were two Lime Kiln fields and one Lime Pit as well as lime kilns in the parish.[123] A lease of the Hill farm in 1764 required the tenant to bring three or four good wagon loads of 'coals' to the lime kiln on the farm, the resultant lime being spread on the arable.[124] In the mid 18th century a field on the Bronsil estate was called Tynings or Brick ground; perhaps it produced bricks for local use. In 1835 Richard Hooper rented a brick ground from the Eastnor estate.[125]

Occupations in the 19th Century

Throughout the 19th century agriculture and domestic service were the main sources of employment in Eastnor. Over half the fathers of infants baptised between 1813 and 1854 were labourers, presumably agricultural; 11 were farmers. Other parental occupations included Lord Somers's butler, two coachmen and a cook, a bailiff at The Farm and a steward at Bronsil, as well as 3 gamekeepers, 12 servants, 2 porters, and 4 grooms. Some at least of the 12 carpenters and 5 masons were probably employed on the Eastnor estate,

114 S.C. Stanford, *Midsummer Hill, an Iron-Age hill fort on the Malverns* (1981), 20.
115 DCA 3766; Eastnor Castle Mun., Castleditch box; ibid., case 2, bundle B.
116 Eastnor Castle Mun., case 1, bundles 6, 7.
117 DCA 3766; Eastnor Castle Mun., case 1, bundle 12.
118 *Pigot's Dir. Herefs.* (1835).
119 *Kelly's Dir. Herefs.* (1913); Eastnor Castle Estate Office, Hollybush Quarries ledger 1935–43, and cashbooks 1958–71; www.bbc.co.uk/herefordandworcester/content/articles/2008/09/17/malvern hills quarrying new 2008 features.html, accessed 7 February 2012.
120 Hist. MSS Com 9 *Hatfield House* (Salisbury) XIII, p. 204; B.S. Smith, *History of Malvern* (1978), 173–4.
121 HRO, CF50/178, Heref DD 31 (Cal of BL Add Ch 72769).
122 DCA 3766; Eastnor Castle Mun., case 3, bundle 1.
123 www.herefordshire.gov.uk/htt/smrSearch/FieldNamesSearch, accessed 9 February 2012. Although most names on the website are from tithe awards, the source of the Eastnor information is probably the inclosure award of 1813.
124 Eastnor Castle Mun., case 1, bundle. 7.
125 ibid., Bronsil box; ibid., Eastnor Estates box 10, Home Audit to Lammas 1835.

Figure 14 *Hollybush quarry, in use in the early 20th century.*

as may have been the hoop shaver, hurdle maker, lath cleaver, 2 lath binders, and 2 sawyers.[126]

Both the total number and the proportion of agricultural workers decreased during the second half of the century from an average of about 78, between a third and a half of the working population, between 1841 and 1861, to 34 or only *c.* 15 per cent of the working population in 1901.[127] As the number employed on the home farm of the Eastnor estate was never recorded, it is impossible to say how many labourers worked in the parish, but 20 were employed on other farms in 1851 and 1861, 24 in 1881. In 1861 the agricultural workers included 4 farm waggoners and a farm carter, in 1881 a cowman, and in 1901 3 cowmen, a shepherd, and 3 graziers.

The number of domestic servants remained fairly steady, at 30–40, except in 1871 when the presence of Lord Somers's household at the Castle raised their number to 48, 7 of them men, and in 1901 when there was a total of 45, including Lady Henry Somerset's household at the Castle and servants employed at the larger farmhouses. The Castle and other large houses employed 4 or 5 gardeners with assistants and labourers in 1851, rising to 12 in 1901. The Eastnor estate also employed gamekeepers, their numbers peaking at 3 with 4 assistants in 1871. The various woodsmen and woodworkers may also have been employed by the estate; there were 10 including 2 sawyers and 3 hurdle makers in 1851, 11 including 4 hoop-makers in 1861. In 1891 eleven cloggers, most of

126 HRO, CD78/1.
127 Except where otherwise the stated the following paragraphs are based on the census enumerators' books: TNA, HO 107/424/13; HO 107/1975; ibid., RG 9/1808; RG 10/2682; RG 11/2581; RG 12/2051; RG 13/2470.

them from Yorkshire or Lancashire, lodged in the parish; itinerant workers in a craft which continued into the 1930s.[128]

Other craftsmen, such as the blacksmiths, carpenters, and wheelwrights recorded in most censuses, were typical of rural parishes. The three excavators and five working masons, all living near the main Ledbury–Worcester road in 1861, were presumably employed on the railway then being built to Ledbury. The one or two bricklayers and masons recorded in most years probably worked on the Eastnor estate. In 1901 four labourers worked in a quarry, probably at the Gullet or Hollybush, and a lime-burner who lived near the Ledbury road worked at that or another quarry. The railway porter, whose child was baptised in 1865[129], and the engine fitter and coal labourer who lived in the parish in 1881 probably worked in Ledbury.

Working women not employed as domestic servants included the schoolmistress, dressmakers, and milliners. In 1851 four women worked as glove sewers and in 1861 two as 'leather gloveresses'; in 1871 as many as thirteen women were employed in gloving, and there were nine glovers in 1891. Like their much more numerous contemporaries in Ledbury,[130] the Eastnor gloveresses presumably worked for Worcester firms.

The presence of Eastnor Castle and its estate did not necessarily bring trade to local people, although many purchases were made in Ledbury. In the early 1820s Lord Somers bought coals and tiles at Upton-on-Severn (Worcs.); his grocer, tailor, and shoemaker were in Hereford, and his gunsmith in Worcester.[131] Other residents went to market in Ledbury, but in 1867 a carpenter and shopkeeper were listed among the tradesmen of the parish.[132] A Co-operative Society was registered in 1869, only the second one to be founded in the county, but was dissolved in 1887.[133] Its shop seems to have been in the village, near the castle. In 1871 there was also a baker in Hollybush road and a butcher at Hillend.[134] In 1890 there were two grocers, one at Hollybush, but in 1895 one was also a farmer.[135] In 1891, 1901 and 1911 The Stores in the village were occupied by a grocer, who in 1911 was also a baker.[136] Grocers, greengrocers, bakers and stationers had shops in the parish in the earlier 20th century.[137]

From the later 20th century the Eastnor Estate has leased buildings to small businesses. In 2012 these included Roger Oates Floors and Fabrics and the Eastnor Pottery. Land Rover Experience, one of ten such centres of excellence in 4 x 4 driving in the country, was based at the home farm.[138]

128 *Alfred Watkins' Herefordshire*, ed. R. and J. Shoesmith (Logaston Press, 2012), 69.
129 HRO, CD78/2.
130 S. Pinches, *Ledbury: A Market Town and its Tudor Heritage* (2009), 99–102.
131 Eastnor Castle Mun., Eastnor Estates box 10.
132 *Littlebury's Dir. Herefs.* (1867).
133 TNA, FS 8/27/1277.
134 ibid., RG 10/2682, f. 1.
135 *Jakeman & Carver's Dir. Herefs.* (1890); *Kelly's Dir. Herefs.* (1895).
136 TNA, RG 12/2051, f. 80; RG 13/2470, f. 82.; RG 14/15608.
137 *Kelly's Dir. Herefs.* (1913, 1917); *Jakeman & Carver's Dir. Herefs.* (1914).
138 www.malverns.landroverexperience.co.uk, accessed December 2012.

SOCIAL HISTORY

SOCIAL STRUCTURE

From the 13th to the 18th Centuries

BY THE LATE 13TH CENTURY, when their names and holdings were recorded in the bishop's rental, the overwhelming majority of tenants on Eastnor manor were small freeholders, described as tenants by socage (for rent, produce or services) and occupying a total of 51 holdings ranging in size from a few acres to a yardland; there were only 13 customary (unfree) tenants, holding between 4 acres and ½ yardland. The proportion of small freeholders to customary tenants was similar on the nearby manor of Colwall where there were *c.* 107 small freeholdings to 26 customary ones. On the manor of Ledbury Foreign, which included the land between Eastnor and Colwall, there was a higher proportion of customary tenants: 53 to 67 small freeholders. Only on Eastnor of the bishop's five Ledbury area manors were the small freeholders called tenants in socage, but the services owed to the bishop were similar on all five manors. As on the manors of Ledbury Foreign and Bosbury, several tenants, apparently small freeholders, held a few acres by annual renders of fish or 'gifts' and honey.[1]

By 1577, when another detailed rental was made for the bishop,[2] Eastnor was dominated by Francis Clinton of Castleditch, who had acquired nine former freeholds and two customary tenements with 90 a. of land in addition to the two sub-manors of Castleditch and Goodings or Old Court. Several other gentlemen held land in the parish, including John Talbot of Grafton (Worcs.), owner of the Bronsil estate. Another non-resident gentleman, Geoffrey Newport, who held several small free- and copyhold estates, was probably the heir of Robert Newport, a member of a Worcestershire family and son-in-law of Gilbert Talbot who had held Bronsil in 1506.[3] John Walwyn, whose messuage at Howler's Heath was occupied by tenants, owned, and presumably lived at, Massington in Ledbury parish. Gabriel Reed was the son-in-law of Thomas Clinton (d. 1575) and the father of William Reed who leased Bronsil Castle; his unnamed daughter was baptised in Eastnor church in 1572.[4]

1   HRO, AA59A1, pp. 143–7.
2   ibid., AA59A2, ff. 92–103.
3   *Trans Bristol and Glos. Arch. Soc.* lx (1938), 278–80; above, Settlement, Landownership.
4   TNA, PROB 11/58, will of Thomas Clynton; Robinson, *Mansions and Manors of Herefs.*, 189; HRO, MX 334 (microfilm of par. regs.); above, Settlement, Landownership.

The relative wealth of those landowners is shown in 1663 when Thomas Cocks of Castleditch was assessed for the maintenance of the militia at £140, nearly three times the amount of the next largest assessment in Eastnor, that of the non-resident Richard Reed of Bronsil. The next highest assessment (£40) was that of Humphrey Morton, who was also assessed for small sums in Ledbury Borough and Foreign; his house near the northern parish boundary was taxed on 5 hearths in 1665, the same number as the rectory but less than half the 12 hearths at Cocks' large house at Castleditch.[5] Humphrey, then described as a gentleman, died in 1671, leaving four sons to inherit Dugmore farm in Eastnor, and other estates at Mitchell in Ledbury, Callow in Munsley, and Leigh (Worcs.).[6] In 1723 Dugmore farm was settled on Anthony Morton, Humphrey's grandson, and in 1761 Anthony's son, another Anthony, of St John in Bedwardine (Worcs.), conveyed the reversion of Dugmores to John Cocks of Castleditch.[7] By 1756 another member of the Morton family, Francis, had acquired Goldhill farm, south of Castleditch; his widow Elizabeth, or another Mrs Morton, still owned it in 1792.[8]

Another 17th- and 18th-century gentry family descended from Thomas Clinton's daughter Mary, who married Edward Higgins in 1563.[9] Their son Thomas lived at Hillend, a large house south-east of Castleditch, and also had land at Woolpits, on the western parish boundary.[10] The family remained at Hillend, although in 1746 Thomas Higgins conveyed the house and c. 43 a. of land to John Cocks of Castleditch, until the

Figure 15 *Anthony Morton's substantial timber-framed house and garden in 1726. The site is now within the deer park.*

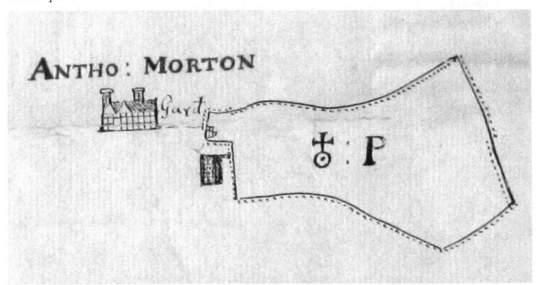

5   *Herefs Militia Assessments* 1663, ed. M.A. Faraday (Camd. 4th ser. x), 96–7, 104; HRO Libr., Transcript of Hearth Tax 1665 by J. Harnden, p. 73; Eastnor Castle Mun., map of Eastnor 1726.

6   HRO, 29/1/44, will of Humphrey Morton 1671; ibid., MX334 (microfilm of par. reg.).

7   Eastnor Castle Mun., case 1, bundle 1A, deeds and papers relating to Dugmores.

8   ibid., case 4, bundle 8, old deeds of Gold Hill estate; HRO, Q/Rel/6/11/3; above, Settlement, Domestic Buildings.

9   HRO, MX334 (microfilm of par. reg.).

10   ibid., 49/3/5: will of Thomas Higgins 1637.

early 19th century.[11] Other members of the family lived elsewhere in Eastnor, one in 1772 holding land on the Bronsil estate.[12] Thomas Higgins of Goldhill died in 1837; his younger brother Joseph (d. 1847), rector of the parish for 52 years, was the last member of the family in Eastnor.[13] By then the dominance of the parish by the Somers Cocks family, the Earls Somers, from their new castle, was complete.[14]

The Somers Cocks family did not spend all their time at Eastnor, having other estates, notably at Reigate (Surrey) which they held from 1758.[15] One attraction of Eastnor is indicated by a lease of 1808 which provided that the tenant of White House farm should keep two sporting dogs for Lord Somers.[16]

The 19th Century

In 1871, when Lord and Lady Somers were in residence, the household at the Castle comprised seven male and eight female servants, including a butler, two footmen, a French chef, a German ladies' maid and three housemaids. In 1901 Lady Henry Somerset, living quietly, employed a secretary, a butler, a footman, and two hall porters, a housekeeper, a cook, a ladies' maid, three housemaids, a laundry maid, a kitchen maid and a scullery maid; her young grandson had a nurse and assistant nurse.[17]

Lady Henry Somerset was Isabella Caroline, the eldest daughter of the third Earl Somers from whom she inherited the Eastnor estate.[18] She married, but later separated from, Lord Henry Somerset. Although she regularly spent time at Eastnor, from where she promoted work among the poor of Ledbury, founding a mission hall in Bye Street, her chief interest was her wider social work, particularly with the Temperance Movement. She became president of the British Women's Temperance Association in 1890 and of the World Christian Temperance Union in 1898. Some of her views, including support for licensed prostitution in certain circumstances, aroused considerable controversy, and she resigned in 1903 to devote herself to work with women alcoholics at a 'colony' founded on her estate in Reigate (Surrey), work which continued until her death in 1921.[19] At Eastnor she established St Mary's Home for Girls c. 1899.[20]

Her successor at Eastnor Castle, Arthur Herbert Tennyson Somers Cocks, sixth Baron Somers (d. 1944), was governor of Victoria, Australia, from 1926 to 1931, but otherwise played an active part in Herefordshire affairs, becoming Lord Lieutenant

11　Eastnor Castle Mun., case 2, bundle B; HRO, Q/Rel/6/11/12; above, Settlement, Domestic Buildings.
12　Eastnor Castle Mun., Bronsil box.
13　Robinson, *Manors and Mansions of Herefordshire*, family tree sv Eastnor [pp. 109–9]. Another branch of the family was established in Bosbury: ibid., 35.
14　Above, Settlement, Landownership
15　*VCH Surrey*, IV, www.british-history.ac.uk, accessed 17 January 2012.
16　Eastnor Castle Mun., case 1, bundle 12.
17　TNA, RG 10/2682, f. 15; RG 13/2470, f. 82v.
18　Above, Settlement, Landownership.
19　*Oxford DNB*, s.v. Somerset, Lady Isabella Caroline; Ros Black, *A Talent for Humanity: the life and work of Lady Henry Somerset* (2010); S. Pinches, *Ledbury: a market town and its Tudor Heritage* (2009), 131, 143.
20　Below, this section, Education.

in 1933. The duke and duchess of York, later George VI and Queen Elizabeth, paid a private visit to Eastnor in the mid 1930s, and in 1937 Lord Somers entertained Queen Mary at the Castle when she made an official, four-day, visit to the county. He shared his predecessor's concern for social work, making the Eastnor park available as a site for an unemployed lads' camp in 1933. His particular interest was scouting, and he succeeded Lord Baden Powell as chief scout of Great Britain in 1941 and of the Commonwealth and Empire in 1942.[21]

CONTACTS BEYOND EASTNOR

Throughout the Middle Ages Ledbury men held land in Eastnor, and Eastnor men, like Adam Pare, who witnessed a charter relating to land in Lilly Hall *c.* 1225, were involved in Ledbury.[22] The bishop's rental of *c.* 1288 records that Eastnor men held a house and a market stall in Ledbury borough.[23] Other Eastnor landholders came from further afield: in 1333 a Hereford man sold land in the parish to a Ledbury man. Richard Walwyn of Lugwardine, presumably a member of the family which held Massington, dealt with land in Eastnor in 1417.[24]

Contacts across the county boundary, particularly with Worcestershire, were frequent. Several men surnamed Malvern or Little Malvern held land in Eastnor in the 13th century.[25] Joan Taylor of Eastnor married a Little Malvern man before 1481.[26] A Great Malvern man was a trustee of a settlement of the Tomblins family lands in Eastnor and Ledbury in 1677, and in 1700 Joseph Baylis of Great Malvern was trustee of an Eastnor marriage settlement.[27] In 1816 a poor boy from Eastnor was apprenticed to a shoemaker in Malvern.[28] Other Worcestershire contacts included a widow of Tenbury (Worcs.) who in the late 14th century had right of dower in Eastnor land.[29] In 1575 two Worcestershire men, from Hanley Castle and Great Malvern, were accused of killing William Branch at Eastnor.[30] Thomas Branch of Eastnor, who died in 1635, had a sister and a cousin in Worcester.[31] In 1638 an Eastnor yeoman's son was established as a clothier in Worcester, and in 1671 a member of the Weobley family of Eastnor was a felt-maker in Upton-on-Severn.[32] John Ford, who died at Eastnor in 1609, seems to have come from nearby

---

21 *Oxford DNB*, s.v. Cocks, Arthur Herbert Tennyson Somers; Hereford City Libr., Newspaper cuttings book no. 5, p. 7 (undated cutting); *The Times*, 12 May, 8 August 1933; 27, 29 July, 2 August 1937; 15, 25 July 1944: from digital archive infotrac.galegroup.com, accessed 4 July 2012.
22 DCA 1751; 3260; ibid., 7018/1, p. 5; BL Add Ch 66626.
23 HRO, AA59/A/1, pp. 131–2.
24 DCA, 7018/3, p. 8; HRO, G37/II/45.
25 e.g. DCA 1763, 3706; HRO, G37/II/87.
26 HRO, CF50/178, Heref A 59 (Cal of BL Add Ch 72880).
27 Eastnor Castle Mun., case 1, bundle 2, no. 13, bundle 3.
28 HRO, CD78/70.
29 ibid., CF50/178, Heref G 29 (Cal of BL Add Ch 72805).
30 *Cal. Pat.* (List & Index Soc.) 1575–8, no. 1, p. 1.
31 TNA, PROB 11/168, will of Thomas Branch.
32 Eastnor Castle Mun., case 2, bundle 1B ; case 4, unnumbered box, bundle 56.

Redmarley (Glos., formerly Worcs.).[33] By 1705 the sisters of an Eastnor weaver had married a husbandman in Stoulton and a carpenter in Hanley Castle.[34]

Contacts with the other neighbouring county, Gloucestershire, seem to have been less close, but a Gloucester burgess made a settlement of land in Eastnor in 1476.[35] In 1679 a Gloucester silk weaver conveyed to a Gloucester spinster a house and land he had inherited in Mitchell. A member of the Weobley family of Eastnor lived in Newent in 1718.[36]

Further afield, one of the Danford family had moved to Welsh Bicknor in Monmouthshire by 1707, and the widow of an Eastnor miller married a Monmouthshire man before 1723.[37] A daughter of Thomas Clinton of Castleditch was married and living in London in 1575 when her father left her two silver gilt spoons, and a sister of the gentleman Thomas Higgins was living in St Bride's, London, in 1746 when both received a legacy from an aunt.[38] Further down the social scale, an Eastnor widow left money to her kinsman in London in 1691, and from the 1770s to *c*. 1800 the two daughters and coheirs of an Eastnor weaver's son lived in Carnaby Market, London. A member of the Weobley family lived in Maidstone, Kent, in 1706.[39]

Throughout the period 1841–91, census records regularly reported that just over half the population of Eastnor had been born in Herefordshire, about a quarter of them in Eastnor itself.[40] Many others came from neighbouring parishes in Gloucestershire and Worcestershire. The proportion of Herefordshire-born inhabitants only went down slightly in 1901 because of the presence of the staff and girls of St Mary's Home, most of whom came from the London area. Many incomers worked for the Eastnor estate, like the land agent from Kent, the drainer from Derbyshire, and probably the mason from Devon in 1851; the gamekeeper from Suffolk and perhaps the builder from Scotland in 1861; the miller from Yorkshire and the gardeners from Leicestershire and Norfolk in 1871; and the lodge porter from Radnorshire and the farm bailiff from Derbyshire in 1881. In 1861 work on the railway line and tunnel in and near the parish attracted miners from Cornwall, Derbyshire, Somerset, and Northamptonshire. A few people were born abroad including the gardener's wife from France in 1851, the park keeper's wife from Italy in 1881, and Hamilton Baillie who lived at Bronsil House in 1871 and 1881 and who was born in India.

33   TNA, PROB 11/115, will of John Ford.
34   Eastnor Castle Mun., case 2, bundle 1B.
35   HRO, CF50/178, Heref P 33 (Cal of BL Add Ch 72875).
36   Eastnor Castle Mun., case 1, bundle 2, unnumbered deeds; case 2, bundle 1B.
37   ibid., case 2, bundles 1B, 6.
38   TNA, PROB 11/58, will of Thomas Clynton; Eastnor Castle Mun., case 2, bundle B.
39   HRO, 114/4/6, will of Jane Alston 1691; Eastnor Castle Mun., case 3, box 1, bundle 25; case 4, unnumbered box, bundle 56.
40   Paragraph based on TNA, HO 107/424; 107/1975; ibid. RG 9/18081; RG 10/2682; RG 11/2581; RG 12/2051.

INNS, RECREATION AND CUSTOMS

A hospice or inn paid rent to the Bronsil estate in 1506, and the inn called Folmers was excluded from the sale of the estate in 1569.[41] The survey of 1578 recorded a hostelry called the New Inn, apparently recently built, on the bishop's manor, and three people kept ale-houses on the manor in 1591.[42] The house in which Thomas Winter allowed 'dancing and other disorders' on the Sabbath in 1609 may also have been an inn or ale house.[43] A house on the main Ledbury to Worcester road, between Hill Farm and Lower Mitchell, called The Cross Hands in 1841, may once have been an inn or beer house although at the time of the census it was occupied by an agricultural labourer and his family.[44] In 1844 Richard Higgins of Goldhill farm was a cider merchant, as in 1859 was Edwin Meacham of White House farm, where the cider mill survived in 2010. Presumably some of the cider was sold in Eastnor, although in 1867 Meacham had a shop in Ledbury High Street.[45]

Figure 16 *The early 19th-century Somers Arms, c. 1920 when it was a substantial hotel.*

41   BL Add MS 46458, f. 26; HRO, CF50/178, Heref R 15 (Cal of BL Add Ch 72905).
42   HRO, AA59 A2, f. 95v.; ibid., AM33/7.
43   *Records of Early English Drama: Herefordshire and Worcestershire*, ed. D.N. Klausner (Univ. Toronto, 1990), 73.
44   TNA, HO 107/424/13, f. 2.
45   *Pigot's Dir. Herefs.* (1844); *Slater's Dir. Herefs.* (1859); *Littlebury's Dir. Herefs.* (1867).

The Somers Arms on Eastnor Hill was so called in 1819, and had been rebuilt, probably as an inn, shortly before that date.[46] In 1871 it was the Somers Arms Hotel, employing three domestic servants; in 1881 the staff included an ostler and a waitress.[47] By 1890, no doubt under the influence of the teetotal Lady Henry Somerset, the Somers Arms had become a temperance hotel and boarding house at which visitors were offered 'every accommodation' including large rooms, tents for parties and stabling for horses.[48] It remained open until the late 1950s, when it was taken over by a racing stables.[49]

In 1922 and 1934 Westfield House, a boarding house at Hollybush, advertised tea rooms and apartments with views of the Welsh mountains and the Cotswold hills. In 1934 and 1937 the Firs, also at Hollybush, provided tea and light refreshments.[50] There was no public house or café in the parish in 2012.

Lady Henry Somerset's work for the village included the establishment of a 'village club' room or hall in 1912. That or another club room, on the main road into the village from Ledbury, was shown on a map of 1926.[51] In 2012 the Eastnor Castle Visitors' Centre was available for use as a community hall.[52] A cricket club established in the 1883 for the estate workers by Lady Henry Somerset, was still active in 2012. It has hosted several famous players, including Basil D'Olivera, for benefit matches. The small, wooden pavilion in Arts and Crafts style, had been built by 1900.[53] Since the late 20th century Eastnor Castle has organised regular events to encourage visitors. An annual summer pop music concert, the Big Chill, held in the Deer Park from 1996 to 2011, attracted great numbers of fans from all over the country.[54]

Local Customs

In the mid 19th century 'wise' men and women in the parish performed witchcraft rituals and healings.[55] In the early 21st century an old oak tree near Ragged Stone Hill was decorated with rags, ribbons and other small objects; the tree was incorrectly

46   HRO, CD78/1: baptisms s.a. 1819; above, Settlement, Domestic Buildings.
47   TNA, RG 10/2682, f. 1v.; RG 11/2581, f. 100v.
48   Jakeman and Carver's *Dir. Herefs.* (1890).
49   Kelly's *Dir. Herefs.* (1941); local information.
50   Kelly's *Dir. Herefs.* (1922, 1934, 1937).
51   Eastnor Castle Mun., Eastnor Parish box, copy of an undated and unattributed essay of *c.* 1980 on the 'Growth of the Village', pp. 30–4; Brooks and Pevsner, *Herefordshire* (2012), 219; OS Map Herefordshire XL11 NW (1931 edn).
52   www.herefordshire.gov.uk/communityhalls, accessed 3 February 2012.
53   Eastnor Castle Estate Office, ledger 1886–9; http://eastnor.play-cricket.com/home/home.asp, accessed 27 January 2012; OS Map 1:2500 Herefs. sheet XLII (2nd edn 1904).
54   www.guardian.co.uk/music/2005/aug/09/popandrock1, accessed 20 October 2012; www.bbc.co.uk/news/uk-england-hereford-worcester-20982953, accessed 15 March 2013.
55   R. Palmer, *Herefordshire Folklore* (Logaston Press, 2002), 92.

identified with the white leaved oak, first recorded in 1584 as one of the boundary marks of Malvern Chase.[56]

EDUCATION

The rector, Richard Coke, by will proved in 1682, bequeathed £5 to apprentice five poor children born in Eastnor. His successor William Stone, by will proved in 1702, instructed his executrix to pay to his successor and the churchwardens and overseers of the poor the sum of £5, the interest from which was to be used to instruct one poor child born in the parish 'in the learning of the English tongue and church catechism'. The money was presumably lost, as in 1716 the rector reported that there was no free school in the parish, although subscriptions had been raised to send 12 children to school the next Michaelmas.[57]

Eastnor School

In 1819 a total of 30–40 children were taught to read at an unspecified number of schools, including a girls' school supported by Lady Somers.[58] Lady Somers's school continued in 1835, when it had 15 pupils; parents paid fees for 8 boys and 12 girls at another day school, and a Sunday School, founded in 1823, taught 22 boys and 44 girls.[59] The two day schools seem to have been amalgamated shortly afterwards. In 1841 a schoolmistress lived near the church, on the site of the later school, whose buildings, designed by Sydney Smirke, were erected in 1845.[60] In 1851 an average of 38 boys and 36 girls attended the schools, which were still supported by Countess Somers.[61] In 1871 there were 61 boys and 43 girls on the roll, and by 1876 the number enrolled had risen to 118, although average attendance was only 80.[62] In 1879 the school could accommodate 133 children; by1886 average attendance had risen to 91.[63] In 1893, probably after Lady Henry Somerset had paid for a new wing, there was accommodation for 159 children and average attendance was 97; by 1905 average attendance had risen to 113.[64]

---

56 http://moelbryn-eastnor.blogspot.com/2005/09/pagap-oak-magic-oak.html, accessed 9 January. 2012; visit 7 January. 2012; Smith, *Hist. Malvern*, 29.

57 TNA, PROB 11/370, will of Richard Coke; PROB 11/467, will of William Stone; HRO, HD5/14/109.

58 *Digest of Returns Select Committee on the Education of the Poor,* HC 224 (1819) ix (1), p. 333.

59 *Abstract of Answers and Returns relative to the State of Education in England,* HC 62 (1835), xli, p. 345.

60 TNA, HO 107/424/13; Eastnor Castle Mun., estate survey, 1840; Brooks and Pevsner, *Herefordshire* (2012), 219.

61 Lascelles, *Dir. Herefs.* (1851).

62 *Return on Elementary Education 1871,* HC 201, p. 32 (1871) lv; Littlebury, *Dir. Herefs.* (1876).

63 *Report of the Committee of Council on Education (England and Wales); with appendix 1879–80* [C.2562-I] HC (1880) xxii; HRO, M5B/16/4; *Report of the Committee of Council on Education (England and Wales); with appendix. 1885–86.* [C.4849-I] HC (1886) xxiv.

64 Kelly's *Dir. Herefs.* (1905).

Figure 17 *Eastnor school, built in 1845, with two schoolrooms; the matching extension on the left was made in 2002.*

From 1862 the school, a parochial one, received a government grant as well as support from the Eastnor estate and the children's pence.[65] The school was leased to the Local Education Authority in 1908, and became a voluntary controlled school in 1952. In the 1930s children travelled to Ledbury for woodwork and domestic science classes, and from 1955 all children aged over 11 were transferred to Ledbury schools. Numbers enrolled at the Eastnor school fell from 68 in 1929 to only 29 in 1960, and in 1983 the school was threatened with closure.[66] By the early 21st century, however, the population of the Ledbury area had grown, and Eastnor Parochial Primary School was often oversubscribed as children travelled to it from outside the parish. A new extension, stone-faced to blend with the older buildings, was opened in 2002, and in 2012 the school had 80 pupils.[67]

65   *Report of the Committee of Council on Education*, [3007] HC (1862), xlii.1; Eastnor Estate Office, ledger 1885–9.
66   TNA, ED 2/29845, ED 16/6853, ED 16/6853; *Hereford Times*, 4 March 1983.
67   TNA, ED 16/6853, HMI Report 2 Nov. 1960; *Hereford Times*, 24 Oct. 2002; www.eastnor. hereford.sch.uk/, accessed 27 January 2012; www.herefordshire.gov.uk/education/schools/CHD_ LedburyPrimarySchool.aspx, accessed 22 October 2012.

St Mary's Home for Girls

The home was established by Lady Henry Somerset as a memorial to her father Earl Somers.[68] The main buildings, designed by Edmund Fisher in roughcast with brick trim and hipped roofs, were erected in 1898–9.[69] In 1900 Lady Henry transferred the home to the Waifs and Strays, later the Church of England Children's Society. In 1901 it housed 24 girls aged between 5 and 16; six of them were being trained for domestic service, the remainder were at school. Most of the girls and the matron came from the London area; none, except the cook, came from Eastnor or elsewhere in Herefordshire.[70] Babies were admitted from 1904, when numbers rose to 30, and boys from 1946. The home, then called Bircham's Grange,[71] closed in 1983. It was converted into an old people's home and remained such in 2012.

THE POOR

Charities

The lands of the poor of the parish of Eastnor were recorded in an indenture of 1715,[72] and in 1716 the rector reported that £5 10s. a year in land had been given by an unknown donor 'for the use of the parishioners.'[73] This benefaction may have been the land belonging to the parish, which was being leased out in 1570, and possibly the land of the church of Eastnor, recorded in deeds of the 13th and the early 16th centuries.[74]

In the 16th and 17th century testators regularly bequeathed small sums to the poor or to the 'poor men's box'.[75] Larger donors included Thomas Clinton of Castleditch who in 1575 left 5 marks (£3 6s. 8d.) to the poor people of Eastnor; Thomas Brooke who in 1616 directed his executors to distribute 6s. to four of the 'godliest poor people', and Margery Parry who in 1655 left £10 to be given away at her funeral.[76]

Thomas Danford the elder, by will dated 1652, bequeathed to the poor of Eastnor £5 as a stock, the income to be distributed annually at Easter at the discretion of the minister, churchwardens, and two other 'discreet men' of the parish. In 1688 William

---

68   Except where otherwise stated the following section is based on www.hiddenlives.org.uk/homes/EASTN01.html, accessed 17 January 2012. This gives a foundation date of 1884, but the home does not appear in the 1891 census: TNA, RG 12/2051.

69   Brooks and Pevsner, *Herefordshire*, 219.

70   TNA, RG 13/2470.

71   HRO, Y51.

72   Eastnor Castle Mun., case 2, bundle 1A.

73   HRO, HD5/14/109.

74   ibid., B38/1; ibid. AH82/15; ibid., CF50/178, Heref Y 9 (Cal of BL Add MS 46458, f. 26); ibid., AA59 A2, f. 96v.

75   e.g. ibid., 44/2/10, will of Robert Webley 1549; 9/3/72, will of Richard Branche, 1597; 97/1/9, will of Henry Aston 1680; TNA, PROB 11/115, will John Ford 1609.

76   TNA, PROB 11/58, will of Thomas Clynton; PROB 11/278, will of Margery Parry; HRO 23/2/8, will of Thomas Brooke 1616.

Norbury was ordered to repay the money to the churchwardens and overseers of the poor to be used in accordance with Danford's will.[77] There is no later record of the charity, which was presumably lost.

It was claimed in the late 18th century that Richard Underwood, by deed dated 1644, had given a rent charge of £1 a year to the poor of Eastnor, and that in 1716 the money had been distributed yearly to householders. The charity had been lost by the early 19th century, but the then Earl Somers accepted that the sum was charged on his estate and undertook to pay it annually to the churchwardens.[78] The earls assisted the poor in other ways. Accounts show that between 1814 and 1820 Lord Somers, in addition to supporting aged workers on his estate, gave to the Eastnor poor 9s. 3d. worth of bread and beef a week, and at Christmas he gave an additional £7.[79]

In addition to the 6s. to the poor mentioned above, Thomas Brooke in 1616 left 6s. to the poor in the church house, apparently mainly widows,[80] suggesting that the house was being used as a poor house. A child was born at the 'poor house' in 1814 and one at the 'parish house' in 1819. All three references, and perhaps others to the church or churchyard cottage housing old people in 1830 and 1835, may be to the cottage which in 1816 stood beside the road on land taken from the churchyard.[81]

Poor Relief before 1834

Their accounts show that between 1815 and 1826 the overseers of the poor paid weekly allowances to the poor, presumably in their own homes as there is no record of a workhouse. The total amount paid fluctuated between £180 and £190 until 1819 when it fell to £138. For the remainder of the period the allowances totalled between £89 and £100 a year. Other people received occasional relief in kind, such as the coals supplied to one pauper in 1816 and the kettle to another the following year. There were several payments for funerals, and one, more unusually, for 'a ring and licence' for the marriage of a pauper's daughter in 1817. From 1827 an annual subscription was paid to Ledbury Dispensary and an annual fee to Congreve Selwyn, a Ledbury surgeon. In 1828 lunatics were sent to Gloucester asylum.[82] The total cost of poor relief fell fairly steadily from £288 in 1816 to £160 in 1825. It rose to £204 in 1827, then rose sharply to £265 in 1828, but fell back to £195 in 1829. Expenditure peaked again at £275 in 1833, but then fell steadily to £202 in 1836. From 1818 onwards an overseer was paid a

77   TNA, PROB 11/238, will of Thomas Danford; ibid., C 93/37/25.
78   *Reports of the. Commissioners for inquiring concerning Charities* (1819–37), p. 111: copy in HRO library; HRO, HD5/14/109.
79   Eastnor Castle Mun., Eastnor Estates box 10.
80   HRO, 23/2/8, will of Thomas Brooke 1616.
81   ibid., CD78/1; CD78/8; ibid., Q/Rel17.
82   ibid., CD 78/70; for Selwyn *see* S. Pinches, *Ledbury a market town and its Tudor heritage*, 93–4.

'salary of £5 a year.[83] From 1834 Eastnor formed part of Ledbury Poor Law Union, and paupers were sent to the Union Workhouse in Ledbury.[84]

83   HRO, CD78/70.
84   F. Youngs, *Local Administrative Units, Northern England* (Royal Hist. Soc., 1991), p. 671, www. visionofbritain.org.uk/relationships.jsp?u_id=10068046&c_id=10001043, accessed 24 January 2012; www. workhouses.org.uk/Ledbury/, accessed 29 May 2013. (Eastnor is omitted from the list of parishes in Ledbury Union).

PAROCHIAL ORGANISATION

THERE WAS A CHURCH in Eastnor by the mid 12th century. The first documentary evidence is the appearance of William, priest of Eastnor, among the witnesses to grants by the bishop of Hereford between 1144 and 1148, and a Norman font of similar date was found underneath the nave floor in 1851.[1] The church originated as a daughter church of the minster at Ledbury: in 1460 its incumbent paid a pension to the portioners (or rectors) of Ledbury church, and in the late 16th century the portioners of Upper and Lower Hall in Ledbury received two-thirds of the tithe of corn of Eastnor.[2] The ecclesiastical parish boundaries were the same as those of the civil parish until 1912 when a small area on the eastern boundary was taken into the new chapelry of Hollybush in the diocese of Worcester.[3]

The bishop of Hereford was patron of the living until 1785 when he exchanged the advowson, with the manor, with Lord Somers for land in Little Marcle.[4] The advowson has since descended with the manor and castle in the Somers Cocks family.

Endowment

In 1291, and again in 1428, the living, a rectory, was one of the poorer ones in the deanery, being assessed for clerical taxation at only £5 13s. 4d.[5] It was valued at £7 19s. 5d. in 1535, being again one of the poorer livings in the deanery.[6] The income was derived from glebe land and the rector's one-third of the tithes. When the tithe was commuted in 1842, an annual rent-charge of £367 7s. was assigned to the rector.[7] The rector's land, presumably glebe, was recorded from 1272.[8] In 1838 the glebe comprised

1   *English Episcopal Acta vii. Hereford 1079–1234,* ed. J. Barrow (British Academy, 1993), pp. 27–8; RCHM, *Herefs.* ii, 74; information sheet in church.
2   *Reg. Stanbury,* 192; Somers-Cocks, *Eastnor and its Malvern Hills,* 206 (transcript of glebe terrier); for Ledbury church, S. Pinches, *Ledbury: people and parish before the Reformation* (2010), 33–4.
3   Kelly's *Dir. Herefs.* (1913); *London Gazette,* 28 June 1912, pp. 4655–6.
4   Eastnor Castle Mun., case 1, bundle 9.
5   *Taxatio Ecclesiastica AD 1291* (Record Commission, 1802), 160; *Inquisitions and Assessments relating to Feudal Aids* (HMSO), ii. 403.
6   *Valor Ecclesiasticus temp Henry VIII* (Record Commission 1810–34), iii. 45; *Reg. Bothe,* 366.
7   TNA, IR 29/14, from microfilm in HRO.
8   HRO, CF50/178, Heref FF 29 (Cal of BL Add Ch 72818), Heref H 6 (Cal of BL Add Ch 72699); DCA 582; ibid., 7018/3, p. 5.

61 a., worth £67 a year.[9] In 1885 the gross value of the living, including 59 a. of glebe, was £419 a year.[10]

In 1397 the rectory house was ruinous.[11] About 1580 the house with its outbuildings, garden, orchard, and fishpond, stood next to the churchyard, probably on the south side of the church as it did in the early 19th century. The house, as described in a probate inventory, then comprised a hall and parlour and one or more small chambers.[12] In 1702, when another inventory was taken, there were a kitchen, parlour and buttery on the ground floor with chambers over them, a cider house with a chamber over it, an 'old kitchen' apparently in an outhouse, a millhouse and a barn.[13] In 1848 the curate in charge of the parish was to live in a house ½ mile from the church, perhaps because the rectory house was not in a fit condition for him. A new rectory house, designed by Sir George Gilbert Scott in plain late Gothic style, was built in 1849–50 on glebe land west of the church.[14]

PASTORAL CARE AND RELIGIOUS LIFE

The Middle Ages

The list of known medieval rectors starts with Adam who witnessed a grant dated to between 1219 and 1231.[15] Despite the relative poverty of the living, several rectors were distinguished, or members of the local knightly class. Robert, rector in about the mid 13th century, held land in Eastnor and Massington with which he was able to dower his daughter, Isabel, on her marriage into a minor Gloucestershire land-owning family.[16] Master John Cantorinus, probably a Savoyard and formerly physician to Bishop Peter de Aigueblanche of Hereford, was rector in 1275. That year he had permission from Bishop Cantilupe to let out his Eastnor benefice for five years while he went on crusade, provided he arranged for a suitable curate to serve the parish and gave ½ mark (6s. 8d.) a year to the poor.[17] Cantorinus was still rector in 1277 when, perhaps because he was abroad, he was one of many clergy who failed to attend an ordination at Leominster, but he died or resigned before 1283.[18] Master Thomas de Boleye or Balleye, rector 1322–c. 1332, acted as proctor for the dean and chapter of Hereford in a dispute with the former archdeacon of Shropshire in 1324. In 1332 he was appointed to try a suit for divorce, not

9   TNA, IR 18/3030.

10   Kelly's *Dir. Herefs.* (1885).

11   A.T. Bannister, 'Visitation Returns of the Diocese of Hereford in 1397', *English Historical Review* xlv (1930), 93.

12   Somers-Cocks, *Eastnor and its Malvern Hills*, 196, 207 (transcript of glebe terrier).

13   TNA, PROB 4/22662.

14   HRO, HD8/24; ibid., CD78/27; Q/R1/17; National Heritage List 1349535 (Eastnor Court).

15   *English Episcopal Acta. Hereford 1234–75* ed. J. Barrow (British Academy, 2009), p. 170.

16   DCA 7018/3, pp. 10–11.

17   *Reg. Cantilupe*, 6–7; *English Episcopal Acta xxxv. Hereford 1234–75*, p. lxxvii; ibid., no. 50, p. 54; ibid., App 5, p. 199.

18   *Reg. Cantilupe*, 302; *Reg. Ric. Swinfield*, 15, 524.

apparently between his own parishioners.[19] In 1424 Michael Morris, rector of Eastnor, acted on behalf of the vicar of Burghill in a dispute with Llanthony priory (Gwent). Richard Belmer, bishop of Achonry in Ireland from 1426 till his death in 1436, was presented to Eastnor in 1429.[20]

Several rectors were non-resident for at least part of their incumbencies. John Huband, who served from 1308 to 1322, had leave in 1312 to be absent to study for three years, and in 1348 Thomas de Brokenhull had leave of absence for two years to attend the bishop of Winchester.[21] In 1356 Henry of Withington had a similar licence for an unspecified reason,[22] perhaps to return to Withington, for in 1363 he and Henry Smith of Withington acknowledged a large debt of 60 marks (£40) to Master Michael of Northborough, prebendary of Church Withington.[23] In 1397 the parishioners reported to Bishop Trefnant that the rector did not reside in the parish.[24] Richard Smith, Bachelor of Canon Law, rector 1511–16, had been vicar of Ledbury from 1479 and was a prebendary of Hereford Cathedral;[25] it seems unlikely that he served Eastnor himself. His successor, William Bolton (1516–18), who was presented by Henry VIII during a vacancy of the see of Hereford, was also prior of St Bartholomew's, in Smithfield, London and master of the king's works; during his tenure of Eastnor he directed works at Hampton Court (London) and New Hall (in Boreham, Essex).[26]

Other rectors grew physically unable to carry out their duties. In 1380 the bishop appointed the rector of Upper Hall in Ledbury and his chaplain co-adjutors to the rector of Eastnor, the rector (probably Thomas Grauntpee presented in 1369) being 'debilitated in limb, sick in body and out of his senses'. A new rector was inducted the following year.[27] In 1417 William Oldford resigned because his bodily weakness made him unable to serve; the bishop assigned him a pension of 5 marks (£3 6s. 8d.) a year out of the benefice, significantly reducing his successor's income. Thomas Hornsey received the same pension on his resignation in 1524.[28]

There is little evidence for minor cults in the medieval church. As in all churches, the Virgin Mary was honoured: in 1332 Thomas Martin endowed a wax light before the statue of the Virgin Mary of Eastnor, and in 1349 and in the early 16th century land of 'St Mary of Eastnor', was mentioned in deeds.[29] Land given to endow a light before the rood, the cross above the chancel arch, was confiscated at the Reformation.[30] Other land

19   DCA 2991; *Reg. Thomas Charlton*, 14.
20   *Reg. Spofford*, 55, 356; www.gcatholic.com/dioceses/diocese/acho0.htm, accessed 27 February 2012.
21   *Reg. Ric. Swinfield*, 545; *Reg. Trillek*, 395, 405.
22   *Reg. Trillek*, 397.
23   *Cal. Close 1349–54*, 591; *Fasti Ecclesiae Anglicanae 1300–1541*, ii, 17.
24   Bannister, 'Visitation Returns', *English Historical Review* xlv. 93.
25   *Reg. Mayew*, 279; A.B. Emden, B*iographical Register of the University of Oxford to AD1500* (1957–9), 1718.
26   *Reg. Mayew*, 285; Emden, *Biographical Register of the University of Oxford AD 1501 to 1540* (1974), 56; H.M. Colvin, *History of the King's Works* (1963–82), iv. 128, 172.
27   *Reg. Gilbert*, 19; DCA 1163.
28   *Reg. Lacy*, 4; *Reg. Bothe*, 336.
29   HRO, CF50/178, Heref C 17 (Cal of BL Add Ch 72727), Heref H 91 (Cal of BL Add Ch 72747); Eastnor Castle Mun., Castle Ditch box.
30   *Cal. Pat* (List & Index Society) 1572–5, no. 2382, pp. 408–9.

held by the church, recorded from the 13th century, may have been given to endow other statues or lights.[31]

Some of the clergy recorded in medieval Eastnor, who were apparently not rectors, may have served subsidiary altars or chantries. Sir Robert, chaplain of Eastnor, who witnessed a charter between 1230 and 1234, may have been one such. William chaplain of Eastnor, who witnessed a deed about the mid 13th century, held land in Eastnor,[32] and may have lived there at least partly on his own resources. In 1350 Sir John the priest of Eastnor was to induct the new rector.[33] Chaplains were recorded in 1389, in 1405, and in 1523 or 1524.[34] Some of them may have served altars in Ledbury church, like Thomas Pontesbury, chaplain of St Anne's chantry in Ledbury, who held a windmill on the bishop's Eastnor manor in 1467. The same rental recorded that an acre in 'le Seche' had once been held by 'Grene hermit'.[35]

John of Eastnor was one of three 'contumacious persons', presumably Lollards, against whom the bishop sought the aid of the secular authorities in 1383, but the parishioners reported no heresy in the parish in 1397.[36]

After the Reformation

Christopher Walwyn, a Cambridge graduate and presumably a member of the gentry family who held Massington, served the church throughout the Reformation period, from 1524 probably until 1573 or 1574. As he obtained the degree of Bachelor of Canon Law in 1519, he must have been growing old by the end of his incumbency, and by 1568 he seems to have been assisted by a curate.[37] The wills written during his time suggest a moderate Protestantism or at least compliance with changing laws.[38] He was followed in 1574 by William Clinton, brother of Thomas Clinton of Castleditch, who was presented by his brother-in-law Thomas Bradley on a grant of the advowson from the bishop.[39]

Thomas Clinton of Castleditch himself was suspected in 1564 of harbouring former Marian (Catholic) clergy, and his name was put forward in 1574 as a potential supporter of Mary, Queen of Scots.[40] His grandson, Ivo Clinton, was associated with the Catholic

31   DCA 7018, p. 21; HRO, AH82/15; ibid. B38/1; ibid. CF50/178, Heref Y 9 (Cal of BL Add MS 46458, f. 26).

32   *English Episcopal Acta, Hereford 1234–75*, App 1, no. xi; DCA 7018/3, pp. 9–10; ibid., 1726.

33   *Reg. Trillek*, 383.

34   HRO, CF50/178, Heref II 29 (Cal of BL Add Ch 72794), Heref G 65 (Cal of BL Add Ch 72814); ibid., AM33/15.

35   BL Add MS 46458, f. 6.

36   *Reg. Gilbert*, 34; Bannister, 'Visitation Returns', *English Historical Review* xlv, 93.

37   *Reg Bothe*, 336; J. and J.A. Venn, *Alumni Cantabrigienses to 1714* (1922–7), 1567; *Calendar of Probate and Administration Acts 1407–1550 in the Consistory Court of the Bishops of Hereford*, ed. M.A. Faraday (2008), p. 386.

38   HRO, 6/5/10, will of John Bache 1545; 12/2/20, will of William Clifton 1565; 23/1/33, will of Jane Hopley 1565; 36/3/7, will of James Rogge 1545; 40/1/53, will of Roger Tarte 1564; 44/2/10, will of Robert Webley 1549; 44/2/26, will of Thomas Webley 1564.

39   HRO, AL19/15, f. 24v.; TNA, PROB 11/58, will of Thomas Clynton.

40   'A collection of original letters from the bishops to the Privy Council', ed. Mary Bateson, Camden Miscellany ix. (Camden 1893). 10; *Miscellanea* (Catholic Record Society xiii), 15.

Russell family of Little Malvern Court, and Richard Cocks seems to have been part of the same circle,[41] but apparently neither of them was a recusant. The only recorded recusant in the parish was a yeoman, John Hill, fined in 1592 or 1593.[42]

William Clinton's successor as rector, William Saintbarbe (d. 1619), came of a Somerset and Wiltshire gentry family, and probably owed his presentation to Eastnor church to his association at Christ Church, Oxford, with the future bishop of Hereford, Herbert Westfaling.[43] He held the degree of Bachelor of Divinity, and his library reflected his learning and interests: at his death it included books by St Augustine, St Thomas Aquinas, Gregory the Great and Irenaeus, as well as historical works by Livy and Plutarch, and 'Stow's *Chronicle*', perhaps part of the two volumes published by Raphael Holinshed.[44] It was probably during his incumbency that the husbandman John Weobley the elder combined old and new ideas in his will, calling Jesus Christ 'our alone saviour and redeemer' but also referring to 'the company of the heavenly angels and blessed saints'.[45]

Richard Coke, rector 1644–82, was presented by his father Bishop George Coke (d. 1646). The living was sequestrated late in 1656 or early in 1657, and in March 1657 H. Walwyn, possibly Humphrey Walwyn, was admitted. Coke was reinstated at the Restoration, for he was rector in the 1670s, although the church was actually served by curates;[46] he was also chancellor of Hereford diocese until 1681.[47] Coke was unpopular with at least some parishioners, one of whom referred in 1679 to the 'lying lips and deceitful tongue of that proud and perjured priest' and hoped that 'his place may be supplied by a man of care and conscience and of an exemplary life and conversation'.[48] Despite such opposition to the rector, the Compton census of 1676 recorded 100 conformists and only 7 nonconformists in the parish.[49] At his death in 1682 Coke asked to be buried in the chancel of Eastnor church, and left money to apprentice five poor children of the parish.[50] His successor William Stone, who had been his curate, seems to have been a local man, perhaps from Bromsberrow, Glos.[51]

The 18th and 19th centuries were remarkable for three long incumbencies: those of John Treherne, Joseph Higgins and William Pulling. Treherne served the church for 52 years, from 1701 to 1753. By 1751 he seems also to have been serving Redmarley D'Abitot (Glos., formerly Worcs.) as well as Eastnor.[52] William Skinner, rector 1766–95, held the rectory of Brasted, Kent, in plurality from 1784, but employed curates to serve that parish

41 *Little Malvern Letters*, i. 1482–1737, ed. A. M. Hodgson and M. Hodgetts (Catholic Record Society lxxxiii), 89, 91.
42 *Recusants Exchequer Roll 1592-3* (Catholic Record Society xviii), 138.
43 *Visitation of Wiltshire 1623* (Harleian Society); *Oxford DNB*, s.v. Herbert Westfaling.
44 J. Foster, *Alumni Oxoniensis 1500–1714*, s.v. St. Barbe; TNA, PROB 11/133, will of William Saintbarbe.
45 HRO, 64A/2/13, will of John Webley the elder 1614.
46 ibid., HD5/1/21–3; *VCH Worcs.* iv. 354–61; A.G. Matthews, *Walker Revised* (Oxford 1948), 192.
47 *Hereford Cathedral: A History*, ed. G. Aylmer and J. Tiller (Hambledon, 2000), 640.
48 HRO, 60/2/22, will of Robert Higgins 1678.
49 *Compton Census*, ed. A. Whiteman, 260.
50 TNA, PROB 11/370, will of Richard Coke.
51 HRO, HD5/1/23; TNA, PROB 11/467, will of William Stone.
52 MI in church (copied in Herefs. Family Hist. Soc. 'Monumental Inscriptions Survey: Eastnor', p. 40); TNA, PROB 11/803, will of John Traherne.

at least part of the time.[53] Joseph Higgins, a member of a long-established Eastnor family descended from the Clintons, served for another 52 years, from 1795 to 1847. From 1808 he held Pixley in plurality with Eastnor.[54] In 1716 and 1719 Treherne, who had been chaplain to Bishop Gilbert Ironside (d. 1701), was resident in Eastnor; he said morning and afternoon prayers on Sundays, with one sermon, and held Communion services four or five times a year.[55] In the 1810s and 1820s Holy Communion was celebrated three or four times a year, usually at great festivals. Higgins was assisted by a licensed curate in 1844.[56]

Higgins's age, and perhaps infirmity, provided an opportunity for Wesleyan Methodists from Ledbury to expand into Eastnor. Houses at Way End Street were licensed for worship in 1839 and 1841, and membership grew from 15 in 1839 to 26 in 1843. The congregation was last recorded in 1846 when there were 23 members. Thereafter Eastnor Methodists presumably worshipped at Ledbury chapel, whose trustees c. 1850 included two Eastnor men.[57]

William Pulling, Higgins's successor, lived in Oxford, where he was a fellow of Brasenose College, until 1851; in 1848 and from 1850 until his death in 1894, he, like Higgins, held Pixley in plurality with Eastnor.[58] In 1851 the pattern of services seems to have been similar to that of the 18th century: morning and evening prayer each Sunday,[59] but thereafter Eastnor experienced the revival in church life common in the later 19th century. Pulling was responsible for rebuilding the rectory house in 1849-50,[60] and the church in 1851–2. From 1854 he employed an assistant curate for Eastnor and Pixley,[61] and in the late 1880s and early 1890s, perhaps because of ill health, a curate in charge.[62] He was one of the compilers and financial supporters of *Hymns Ancient and Modern*,[63] suggesting a moderate high churchmanship. A processional cross with the figure of the crucified Christ presented by Caroline, Countess Somers (d. 1852), was believed to be the first such cross used in an English country church; it was replaced by an elaborate, jewelled cross given by Lady Henry Somerset in 1900. By 1901 the church was equipped with altar frontals in liturgical colours. The choir of men and boys, recorded in 1870, was apparently the first surpliced parish choir in Herefordshire. There was an organ by 1854 when the

53 Foster, *Alumni Oxoniensis*, 1715–1886, 1304; www.theclergydatabase.org.uk/jsp/persons/DisplayPerson.jsp?PersonID=37610, accessed 6 August 2011.

54 http://melocki.org.uk/diocese/Pixley.html, accessed July 2011.

55 HRO, HD5/14/109; HD5/15/35; MI in church.

56 HRO, CD78/70; ibid., Card index to Diocesan Year Boxes.

57 ibid., HD8, Annual boxes 1839, 1841/2: meeting house licences; ibid., AC93/33: Ledbury Wesleyan Methodist Circuit book; TNA, HO 107/424/13, f. 17; HO 107/1975, f. 81v.

58 HRO, card index to Diocesan Year Boxes; plaque on desk (copied in Herefs. Family Hist. Soc. 'Monumental Inscriptions Survey: Eastnor', p. 44); Foster, *Alumni Oxoniensis* 1715–1886, 1163.

59 HRO, HD10/4.

60 ibid., CD78/27.

61 ibid., HD10/6; ibid., index to Diocesan Year Boxes 1857, 1860, 1863. Somers-Cocks, *Eastnor and its Malvern Hills*, 222,

62 HRO, CD78/62; TNA, RG 12/2051, f. 83v.

63 Somers-Cocks, *Eastnor and its Malvern Hills*, 221; *Hymns Ancient and Modern* (Hymns Ancient and Modern Ltd, 2011).

churchwardens paid bills for it; in 1867 Earl Somers gave a new one which was still in the church in 2012.[64]

James Dennis Hird, rector 1894–6, had been organising director of the London diocesan branch of the Church of England Temperance Society, a cause strongly espoused by the patron of the living, Lady Henry Somerset. He was a prolific author of theological, scientific, and social books, including *Health, Wealth and Temperance* (1890) and *Jesus the Socialist: a lecture* (1896), but was later accused of atheism.[65] In 1901 a 'Church of England evangelist' lived at Way End Street.[66] From 1901 or earlier until 1903 monthly services were held at Hollybush, and an open-air service was held there in 1910.[67]

For much of the 20th century the pattern of Sunday services at Eastnor remained the same: an early service of Holy Communion followed by Mattins, with Communion once a month, and then Evensong.[68] H.L. Somers Cocks, uncle of the sixth Baron Somers and a cousin of Lady Henry Somerset, took occasional services from 1901 and was rector from 1915 to 1929. E.C. Elliott, rector from 1932 to 1959, seems to have been rather more Evangelical than his predecessors, and during his incumbency the number of weekday Communion services was reduced. His successor, R.C. Moore, introduced a quarterly Choral Communion and a midnight Communion at Christmas.[69] From 1973 Eastnor was held in plurality with Ledbury, and in 1998 the parish became part of the Ledbury Team ministry.[70]

THE CHURCH OF ST JOHN THE BAPTIST

The church is dedicated to St John the Baptist.[71] It has a chancel with north aisle and north chapel, nave with north aisle and south porch, and a west tower. All except the tower was rebuilt under the direction of Sir George Gilbert Scott in 1851–2.[72] The earliest features in the medieval church, apart from the Norman font, were the late 12th-century south door, reused by Scott, and perhaps the chancel arch, said by H.L. Somers-Cocks,

64   HRO, CD78/2, baptisms 1870; CD78/62; Somers-Cocks, *Eastnor and its Malvern Hills*, 224–9; Hereford City Libr., Pilley colln. 2280, p. 50; ibid., C.M. Beddoe colln. of church prints, vol. 2, p. 57. Littlebury's *Dir. Herefs.* (1876).

65   *The Times*, 6 April 1894, from digital libr. accessed through Herefordshire Libraries, Sept. 2011; Bodleian Libr. catalogue at http://library.ox.ac.uk, accessed November 2011; *Oxford DNB* s.v. Henry Sanderson Furniss (1868–1939).

66   TNA, RG 13/2470, f. 88.

67   HRO, CD78/21, 78/62.

68   ibid., CD78/21–6; CL23/5/1 (Deanery magazines).

69   *Hereford Diocesan Year Books*, 1929–80; *Crockford's Clerical Directory* 1933, ibid., 1955–6.

70   Inf. from The Revd Paul Dunthorne, Team Rector, Ledbury Team Ministry.

71   Dedication first recorded c. 1852: Hereford City Libr., C.M. Beddoe colln. of Church Prints, vol. 2, pp. 56–7. Slater's *Dir. Herefs.* (1859) gives the dedication as Christ Church. A reference in an early 16th-century rental to 'land of St Mary of St. Mary of Eastnor', if it is not a scribal error, suggests that the medieval dedication was to St Mary: Eastnor Castle Mun., Castle Ditch box (17th-century copy of account of lands called Dychons).

72   Description based on RCHME *Herefs.* ii. 73–4; National Heritage List 1266756; Brooks and Pevsner, *Herefordshire* (2012), 218–19; Somers-Cocks, *Eastnor and its Malvern Hills*, 174–7; *Herefordshire Churches through Victorian Eyes*, ed. J. Leonard (Logaston Press, 2006), 43.

on the basis of sketches by Sir George Gilbert Scott borrowed from the architect's firm, to have had imposts 'of Norman character'; so the 12th-century church probably had comprised a nave and chancel. The north aisle, which contained two lancet windows, was added in the 13th century; its west window inserted in the 14th century. The arcade seems to have been altered in the 15th century. (The late 12th-century materials in the rebuilt arcade may be from the original chancel arch.) The two lower stages of the tower were built in the 14th century; it was remodelled and a third stage added in the 15th century. Major repairs or rebuilding, for which indulgences were granted in 1455 and 1475, probably included the building of the north chancel chapel, which was described by Somers-Cocks as having been 'perpendicular',[73] and the upper stage of the tower.

The chancel arch and part of the arcade between the chancel and the north chapel were rebuilt and widened during the 18th century.[74] Further repairs were carried out in 1824 when the churchwardens spent just over £77 on the fabric, including £26 4s. 9½d. for the mason's bill, £15 9s. 6d. for the smith's bill, and £16 3s. for laths, tiles and nails. Before 1846 the nave was repewed 'thanks to the right feeling' of the second Earl and Countess Somers.[75]

Scott rebuilt the church, mainly on its medieval foundations, as a nave with north aisle and south porch, and a chancel with north aisle and a vestry in the angle between the east end of the aisle and the chancel; a mortuary chapel for the Somers Cocks family was added on the north side of the north chancel aisle. The east window and the two south windows of the chancel are of 14th-century style with ballflower ornament. If this reflects the medieval windows, it would place the remodelling of the chancel in the early 14th century, and perhaps associate it with contemporary work on the north chapel of Ledbury church.[76]

The tower was probably repaired in or shortly after 1858, when Scott reported on the 'measures necessary for the security' of the tower. His report was sent to Lord Somers, who presumably paid for the work.[77] In 1893 both the tower and the churchyard wall were giving cause for concern, and an architect's report was to be commissioned.[78] Repairs were presumably carried out by Lady Henry Somerset.The church had a ring of four bells in 1553. All were recast by members of the Rudhall family during the late 17th century and the earlier 18th; a fifth bell was cast in 1745, and a sixth, by Mears and Co. of Whitechapel, was added to the ring in 1864.[79] Two bells were recast by the Whitechapel foundry, and the whole ring rehung in 1967.[80]

Among the monuments to members of the Cocks and Somers Cocks family under the tower and in the north chancel chapel, those to Joseph Cocks (d. 1775) by Thomas Scheemakers to the design of James 'Athenian' Stuart, to the second Earl Somers (d.

73   *Reg. Stanbury*, 19; *Reg. Myllyng*, 206; Somers-Cocks, *Eastnor and its Malvern Hills*, 177.
74   Somers-Cocks, *Eastnor and its Malvern Hills*, 176.
75   HRO, CD78/70; *Herefordshire Churches through Victorian Eyes*, ed. Leonard, 43.
76   S. Pinches, *Ledbury people and parish before the Reformation*, 129.
77   He had paid for the rebuilding of the nave: www.eastnorcastle.com/church.htm, accessed 18 March 2013.
78   HRO, CD78/62.
79   F. Sharpe, *Church Bells of Herefordshire* i (Brackley, 1969), 146–8; Somers-Cocks, *Eastnor and its Malvern Hills*, 230; HRO, CD78/62.
80   HRO, CD78/26.

Figure 18 *Eastnor church in 2012, rebuilt more elaborately in 1850–1.*

Figure 19 *The medieval church from the south-east c. 1850. All that survived the rebuilding was the tower and some 12th-century fragments.*

Figure 20 *The Victorian interior of the church. The scalloped capital at the east end of the arcade is one of the 12th-century fragments reused by the architect, G.G. Scott.*

1852) by J.B. Philip to the design of Sir George Gilbert Scott, and to the third earl (d. 1883) by Sir J.E. Boehm to the design of G.E. Fox are particularly notable. The alabaster reredos, installed in 1896 in memory of the rector William Pulling, incorporates parts of a monument from Siena.[81] An oak screen to close off the tower arch and a landing for the bell ringers were installed in 1921, in memory of the rector's son Capt. Reginald Somers Cocks.[82] The plate includes a silver chalice and paten of 1572, given by the rector in 1919, also in memory of his son. The silver gilt chalice and paten of 1853 were made by reusing

81   HRO, HD10/75, Diocesan Annual box 1896 (2); Brooks and Pevsner, *Herefordshire*, 218.
82   HRO, HD10/121, Diocesan Annual box 1921 (2).

the metal from earlier church plate given by the Somers Cocks family in 1840. That earlier plate may itself have reused silver from the parcel gilt chalice recorded in 1553.[83]

The churchyard was enlarged in 1925 by the addition of a strip of glebe land along the south side.[84] In the north-west corner is a covered seat with, against its back, five terracotta relief panels, designed by Lady Henry Somerset and depicting Christ the King, two angels, the Sower and Ceres.[85]

83   Somers-Cocks, *Eastnor and its Malvern Hills*, 227–8.
84   HRO, HD10, Annual box 1925.
85   National Heritage List 1224570; Brooks and Pevsner, *Herefordshire*, 219.

SOURCES USED

THIS VCH HISTORY of Eastnor has been written using a wide range of original documents, some of them printed but most manuscript sources. It is that dependence of primary sources (ie. created at the time under study) which makes VCH histories both new and reliable. The sources are discussed here. The list does not claim to be comprehensive, and so is best used in conjunction with the List of Abbreviations and, where possible, with the online resources mentioned here and below. A very important resource is the website of The National Archives www.nationalarchives.gov.uk, which gives access to detailed catalogues and research guides as well as to references to a selection of material from the Herefordshire Archives through Access to Archives, www.nationalarchives.gov.uk/a2a/ and the National Register of Archives, www.nationalarchives.gov.uk/nra/.

MANUSCRIPT SOURCES

Public Repositories

The **Herefordshire Record Office** holds the records of county government (including inclosure awards and 18th- and 19th-century land tax assessments), the Hereford diocesan and archidiaconal records (including bishops' registers, documents relating to the administration of the bishop's estates and church terriers), and nonconformist records. It also has a large collection of private records including charters and accounts. The principal documents used in this history are:

AA59 A1: a rental of the bishop's manors, *c.* 1288
AA59 A2: survey of the bishop's estates by Swithun Butterfield, 1577
AH82: charters relating to the estates of the bishop of Hereford
AM33: bailiffs' accounts and court records for the bishop's manors, 1497–1592
CD78: Eastnor parish records
CF50/178: Typescript calendar of the Talbot charters in the British Library, relating to the Bronsil estate
G37: medieval charters relating to the Walwyn estate
HD5: 17th-century visitation records, and visitation returns for 1716 and 1719
HD2, HD8, HD10: other diocesan records, mainly relating to parish clergy and parish administration, from the mid 19th century onwards

Q/R1/17: Eastnor inclosure award and map
Q/Rel: Land tax assessments from 1787
Local wills proved in the diocesan court in the 16th and 17th centuries; these are
numbered in the form 9/3/46, with no preliminary letters.

Herefordshire's **Historic Environment Record** (formerly the Sites and Monuments
Record) holds notes of archaeological sites and features and of listed buildings. It is
accessible at Herefordshire Through Time: www.herefordshire.gov.uk/27.aspx.

The **Hereford Cathedral Library** holds the archives of the Dean and Chapter of
Hereford including a large number of charters, a 16th-century cartulary (DCA 7018),
some rentals, and other documents relating to the Eastnor lands of St Katherine's
Hospital, Ledbury.

The National Archives at Kew, London hold the records of national government from
the late 12th century onwards. Calendars of some medieval administrative records which
have been used in this history, notably the Close and Patent Rolls, have been published.
The classes of documents used in this history include:

C 1: Legal proceedings in the court of Chancery, 1386–1558
C 6: Legal proceedings in the court of Chancery 1625–1714
C 93: Inquisitions (Enquiries) and Decrees made by the Commissioners for Charitable
Uses (set up to investigate abuses), 1558–1820
C 142: Inquisitions post mortem (enquiries into the lands held by deceased tenants-in-
chief of the Crown), 1485–1649
C 143: Inquisitions ad quod damnum (enquiries into lands to be granted to the Church),
1216–1485
CP 25/1: Feet of Fines (note of agreements reached in, often fictitious, land disputes),
1195–1509
E 134: Depositions taken from witnesses in suits in the court of the Exchequer, 1558–
1841
E 320: Particulars for sale of the estates of Charles I, 1649–1660
ED 2: Department of Education and its Successor: Elementary Education, Parish Files
ED 16: Board of Education and its Predecessor: Elementary Education, Local Education
Authority Supply Files, 1870–1945
FS 8: Registry of Friendly Societies: Rules etc. of Societies removed from the register after
1874 and before 1913
HO 107: Census Enumerators' returns, 1841, 1851
IR 18/3030: Tithe files, Eastnor, agreement and apportionment, 1836–70
IR 29/14/74: Tithe Commission and its Successors: Eastnor tithe apportionment, 1838
MAF 32: Ministry of Food, National Farm Survey, Individual Farm Records, 1941–3
MAF 37: Ministry of Agriculture and Fisheries, and Ministry of Agriculture, Fisheries
and Food: Crop Production, Correspondence and Papers, 1930–1958
PROB 11: Records of the Prerogative Court of Canterbury, registers of wills proved
1384–1858
RG 9–14: General Register Office, Census Enumerators' returns 1861–1911

SC 6/HenVIII/1511: Special Collections, Ministers' and Receivers' Accounts for estates in the possession of the Crown, Eastnor 1536–1538

London, British Library. The Additional (Add) manuscripts and charters include records of the Talbot family estate, most of which were calendared in the 1930s (see above, Herefordshire Record Office).

Private Archives

Eastnor Castle Muniment Room, to which the VCH team was granted access, contains deeds relating to the Eastnor Castle estate, as well as correspondence, bills, etc. concerning the building of the castle, and a series of estate maps. Some of the maps, including the detailed ones of 1726, have been described by Brian Smith in *Herefordshire Maps 1577 to 1800* (Logaston Press, 2004).

PRINTED SOURCES

Primary Sources

The most important printed primary sources, including calendars of major classes in The National Archives are included in the List of Abbreviations. The *Registers* of Bishops Cantilupe, Orleton, Thomas and Lewis Charlton, Trillek, Courtenay, Gilbert, Trefnant, Mascall, Lacy, Polton, Spofford, Beauchamp, Boulers, Stanbury, Milling, Mayew, and Booth, which were printed by the Cantilupe Society between 1906 and 1921, contain information about Eastnor manor as well as about the church.

Herefordshire Trade Directories, found in the Herefordshire Record Office Library and at www.historicaldirectories.org/hd, include Jakeman & Carver's *Directory* (1890, 1914), Kelly's *Directory* (1885–1941), Lascelles *Directory* (1851), Littlebury's *Directory* (1867, 1876), Pigot's *Directory* (1835, 1844) and Slater's *Directory* (1859, 1868).

The other published primary sources used in this history are:

English Episcopal Acta xxxv. *Hereford 1234–75*, ed. Julia Barrow (British Academy, 2009)
Calendar of Probate and Administration Acts 1407–1550 in the Consistory Court of the Bishops of Hereford, ed. M.A. Faraday (2008)
Herefordshire Militia Assessments 1663, ed. M.A. Faraday (Camd. 4th ser. x)
Herefordshire taxes in the reign of Henry VIII, ed. M.A. Faraday (Woolhope Club, Hereford, 2005)

Books and articles

The most important secondary source for the history of Eastnor is Henry L. Somers-Cocks, *Eastnor and Its Malvern Hills* (Hereford, 1923); it was written by the rector of the parish, who made extensive use of the muniments at Eastnor Castle. J. Hillaby, *St*

Katherine's Hospital Ledbury c. 1230–1547 (Logaston Press 2003) deals in detail with the St Katherine's Hospital estates.

Two 19th-century works on Herefordshire history have been used: M.G. Watkins, *Collections for the History and Antiquities of Herefordshire, Radlow Hundred* (1902, bound as Duncomb's *Herefordshire* vol. 5) and C.J. Robinson, *Mansions and Manors of Herefordshire* (1873, reprinted Logaston Press, 2001).

Guidebooks to *Eastnor Castle* include one by Lady Henry Somerset (1899).

The main sources for architectural history are Alan Brooks and Nikolaus Pevsner, *Herefordshire* (The Buildings of England, 2012) and Royal Commission on Historical Monuments (England), *An Inventory of the Historical Monuments in Herefordshire*: vol. 2 East (HMSO, 1932).

The following abbreviations and short titles have been used.

BL	British Library
Cal	Calendar
Cal. Chart. R.	*Calendar of the Charter Rolls preserved in the Public Record Office* (HMSO, 1903–27)
Cal. Close	*Calendar of the Close Rolls preserved in the Public Record Office* (HMSO, 1892–1963)
Cal. Fine R.	*Calendar of the Fine Rolls preserved in the Public Record Office* (HMSO, 1911–1962)
Cal. Inq. Misc	*Calendar of Inquisitions Miscellaneous (Chancery) preserved in the Public Record Office* (HMSO, 1916–68)
Cal. Pat.	*Calendar of the Patent Rolls preserved in the Public Record Office* (HMSO, 1890–1986)
Cat. Anct D.	*Descriptive Catalogue of Ancient Deeds in the Public Record Office* (HMSO, 1890–1915)
Cur. Reg. R.	*Curia Regis Rolls preserved in the Public Record Office*
DCA	Dean and Chapter Archives, in Hereford Cathedral Library, Hereford
Dir.	*Directory*
EPNS	English Place-Name Society
HER	Historic Environment Record (formerly SMR or Sites and Monuments Record) at Herefordshire through time: htt.herefordshire.gov.uk/
Hist.	History/Historical
Hist. MSS Com.	Royal Commission on Historical Manuscripts
HMSO	His (Her) Majesty's Stationery Office
HRO	Herefordshire Record Office
Libr.	Library
Mun.	Muniments
NMR	National Monuments Record (Swindon)

OS	Ordnance Survey
Oxford DNB	*Oxford Dictionary of National Biography* (Oxford University Press, 2004); www.oxforddnb.com
RCHM	Royal Commission on Historical Monuments (England)
Reg. Bothe	*The Register of Charles Bothe, Bishop of Hereford 1516–1535*, ed. A.T. Bannister (Hereford 1921)
Reg. Cantilupe	*The Register of Thomas de Cantilupe, Bishop of Hereford 1275–1282*, ed. W.W. Capes (Hereford 1906)
Reg. Mayew	*The Register of Richard Mayew, Bishop of Hereford 1504–1516*, ed. A.T. Bannister (Hereford 1919)
Reg. Lacy	*The Register of Edmund Lacy, Bishop of Hereford 1417–1420*, ed. A.T. Bannister (Hereford, 1917)
Reg. Myllyng	*The Register of Thomas Myllyng, Bishop of Hereford 1474–1492*, ed. A.T. Bannister (Hereford, 1919)
Reg. Stanbury	*The Register of John Stanbury, Bishop of Hereford 1453–1474*, ed. J.H. Parry (Hereford, 1918)
Reg. Thomas Charlton	*The Register of Thomas de Charlton, Bishop of Hereford 1327–1344*, ed. W.W. Capes (Hereford, 1909)
Reg. Spofford	*The Register of Thomas Spofford, Bishop of Hereford 1422–1448*, ed. A.T. Bannister (Hereford, 1919)
Reg. Ric. Swinfield	*The Register of Richard de Swinfield, Bishop of Hereford 1283–1317*, ed. W.W. Capes (Hereford, 1909)
Reg. Trefnant	*The Register of John Trefnant, Bishop of Hereford 1389–1404*, ed. W.W. Capes (Hereford, 1914)
Reg. Trilleck	*The Register of John de Trilleck, Bishop of Hereford 1344–1361*, ed. J.H. Parry (Hereford, 1910)
Soc.	Society
TNA	The National Archives
Trans. Bristol and Glos Arch. Soc.	*Transactions of the Bristol and Gloucestershire Archaeological Society*
TS	Typescript
TWNFC	*Transactions of the Woolhope Naturalists' Field Club*

The following technical terms may require explanation. Fuller information on local history topics is available in D. Hey, *The Oxford Companion to Local and Family History* (1996), or online at the VCH website, www.victoriacountyhistory.ac.uk. The most convenient glossary of architectural terms is *Pevsner's Architectural Glossary* (2010), also available for iPhone and iPad.

advowson: the right to nominate a candidate to the bishop for appointment as rector or vicar of a church. Often attached to a manor, but could be bought and sold.

assign: the person to whom property and rights were legally transferred.

bay: in architecture, a unit of a building inside or out regularly divided from the next by features such as columns of windows. Can apply to a window projecting from a bay.

copyhold: form of land tenure granted in a manor court, so called because the tenant received a 'copy' of the grant as noted in the court records. Often given for several lives (e.g. tenant, wife, and eldest child).

customary tenure: unfree or copyhold tenure regulated by local manorial custom.

demesne: in the Middle Ages, land farmed directly by a lord of the manor, rather than granted to tenants. Though usually leased out from the later Middle Ages, demesne lands often remained distinct from the rest of a parish's land.

furlong: a block of strips in the open fields.

hearth tax: royal tax imposed in 1662 and 1665, assessed on the number of hearths or fireplaces in each taxpayer's house.

hide: unit of land measurement: in Bede's time the amount required for a family to subsist on; in Domesday Book (1086), a taxation unit; and by the 13th century the sum of 4 yardlands (q.v.).

hundred: a subdivision of the county or shire, established before the Norman Conquest and nominally containing 100 hides. Hundreds had their own courts.

inclosure: the process whereby open fields was divided into fields, to be redistributed among the various tenants and landholders. From the 18th century usually by an Act of Parliament obtained by the dominant landowners; earlier, more commonly done by private agreement, or by a powerful lord acting on his own initiative.

knight's fee or service: an amount of land capable of providing enough money to provide a knight for a set period of time – almost invariably 40 days – when required, though some fees demanded other kinds of military service, such as an archer or warhorse. Such obligations became monetary or in kind, and by the 13th century as estates were divided up smaller estates could be held as fractions of a knight's fee.

manor: a piece of landed property with tenants regulated by a private (manor) court. Originally held by feudal tenure (see knight's fee), manors descended through a succession of heirs but could be given away or sold.

messuage: portion of land or a holding, generally with a house and outbuildings on it.

open (common) fields: communal agrarian organization under which an individual's farmland was held in strips scattered amongst two or more large fields, intermingled with strips of other tenants. Management of the fields and usually common meadows and pasture was regulated through the manor court or other communal assembly.

parish: the area attached to a parish church and owing tithes to it. From the Elizabethan period it had civil responsibilities, hence a 'civil' as opposed to an 'ecclesiastical' parish. At first the two were usually identical, but from the 19th century, when many parishes were reorganized, their boundaries sometimes diverged.

ploughland: the amount of land possible to plough in a year by a full team of eight oxen; by the 13th century a unit of land measurement, nominally containing four yardlands (q.v.).

prebend: land or other property (including tithes) owned by a cathedral and allocated in perpetuity to one of the cathedral's canons (or 'prebendaries').

quitclaim: a document which performs or confirms the giving up of all claim to a piece of property.

rectory: (a) a church living served by a rector, who generally received the church's whole income; (b) the church's property or endowment (the rectory estate), comprising tithes, offerings and usually some land or glebe.

recusant: a Roman Catholic who did not attend the services of the Church of England, as was required by law.

socage: a feudal duty, usually payment of rent or produce but sometimes official or personal service.

stint: the number of animals a tenant was allowed to graze on the common pastures, dictated by local custom and enforced usually through the manor court.

suit of court: a tenant's obligation to attend the lord's manor court.

terrier: From the Latin *terre* (land). A register of the lands belonging to a landowner, originally including a list of tenants, their holdings, and the rents paid, later consisting of a description of the acreage and boundaries of the property.

tithing: group of ten householders legally responsible for each other's good behaviour and for referring wrongdoers to the manor court.

vestry: (a) in a church where clerical vestments are stored; (b) assembly of leading parishioners and ratepayers, responsible for poor relief and other secular matters as well as church affairs.

vicar: until the 19th century a clergyman appointed to act as priest of a parish, particularly as assistant to or substitute for the rector. He received a stipend or a proportion of the church's income.

yardland: the conventional holding of a medieval peasant, of 15–40 acres depending on local custom. Most generated surplus crops for sale at market, although those with fragments of yardlands probably needed to work part-time for better-off neighbours.

yeoman: from the 16th century, a term used for more prosperous farmers, many of them socially aspirational. The term husbandman usually denoted less well-off farmers.

INDEX

All places are in Herefordshire unless otherwise stated. All buildings, fields, institutions etc. are in Eastnor unless otherwise stated. References to illustrations are in italics.

CPSIA information can be obtained
at www.ICGtesting.com
Printed in the USA
FSHW021629310321
79947FS

9 781905 165964